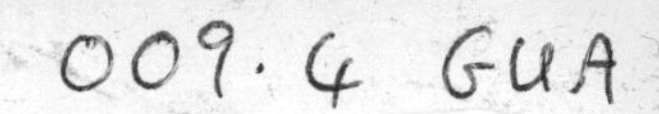

The Guardian Guide To Volunteering

First published by Guardian Books, an imprint of Guardian News and Media.

Written and researched by Tash Banks, Liz Ford and Shiona Tregaskis

A CIP record for this book is available from the British Library.

ISBN: 978-0-85265-067-7

Cover Design: Two Associates
Text Design: Jane Daniel

Printed and bound in Great Britain by William Clowes Ltd, Beccles, Suffolk

Comments/feedback are welcome: please send to brandedbooks@guardian.co.uk.

The Guardian Guide To Volunteering

gb
guardianbooks

CONTENTS

Foreword

With London hosting the Olympic Games and the Paralympic Games in 2012, there's never been a more exciting time for volunteering in the UK. It will take some 70,000 volunteers to make these spectacular global events happen, from sports coaches and translators to caterers, drivers and marshals. And of course the legacy of Olympic volunteering will extend far beyond 2012.

Volunteering has become a powerful force for social change and it is all down to you, the individual. Volunteering empowers you to change the things that you care about, and the range of opportunities on offer means you can choose an experience that meets your specific needs. Remember, volunteering isn't just about what you give but what you can get out of it, from increased career prospects and a new set of friends, to a confidence boost and better health.

TimeBank is constantly dreaming up new and exciting ways to volunteer and our projects address very real needs. When volunteering is a passion not a chore, the impact it has within a community is greater than ever.

TimeBank knows that it can sometimes be tricky to get started with volunteering. We've worked with nearly 250,000 volunteers and they often tell us that they knew their skills were in demand, but they just didn't know where to begin. In fact, 80 per cent of people claim that if volunteering was easier to get into, they'd be doing it with the best of them. This is why TimeBank exists; to give volunteers the inspiration, the support and the opportunities to share time with communities that need them.

TimeBank is proud to be associated with The Guardian Guide to Volunteering, which makes volunteering accessible to everyone. From help with deciding on what you want to do, to tips on how to get started, plus all the practicalities and legalities you need to know about along the way, the Guide is a superb introduction to the world of volunteering.

Whatever your skills and passions, and wherever you choose to apply them, volunteering makes amazing things happen. Every day we witness its power. We see a young man who's battled with low self-esteem sign up to an evening class thanks to the confidence his mentor has built in him. We see a group of classmates get their voices heard thanks to the support they've had to set up a community radio station.

We hope this book gives you the inspiration and the tools to bring your personal visions to life and we wish you the very best of luck with your volunteering.

Moira Swinbank, OBE
Chief Executive of TimeBank

Introduction

Volunteer! it is an old-fashioned word that somehow suggests the opposite – 'You, you and you!' It summons up images of Lord Kitchener's accusatory pointing finger, 'Your country needs you!' It can sound more like duty than pleasure. It smacks of uniforms and bossy people, Joyce Grenfell officiousness and a whiff of boiled cabbage in institutional corridors or digging gardens on wet Sundays. Granny bashing, it used to be called. It is a pity there isn't a better new word than 'volunteer' – but there isn't.

What this guide tells you is how unlike that word it can be. What Granny ever wanted to be bashed by very reluctant school kids, eying the door and longing to be off? Compulsory volunteering isn't the point. The truth is, volunteering only works if it is enjoyable. Somewhere in these pages is something for everyone, something almost anyone would find fun. Forget the idea of the dutiful volunteer smugly doing good to others as a personal sacrifice. If it isn't a two-way win, then it won't work.

That is the great secret. That is why three-quarters of the population did some kind of volunteering at some point in 2006. Even with ever busier lives most people found time because they wanted to. Gone are the old days of vast battalions of women stuck at home looking for something useful to do. Most mothers now work – and yet still find time to volunteer in one way or another. But only because they found something they really enjoyed with people who were congenial company. Otherwise, frankly, most people wouldn't do it. Altruism is a part of the pleasure – but it doesn't take many people beyond the occasional gesture. Finding the right thing for you is what this guide is all about.

Like many people, I was roped into volunteering by a friend. Try this, she suggested, handing me a brochure. I was deeply dubious. Do I have spare time? No, absolutely not. Am I patient and nice? Not particularly. TimeBank's Time Together organises mentors for refugees to give those settling in to Britain a friend who knows the ropes, an adviser, a companion, someone who can answer basic questions about living in a new country. Could I? I thought probably not. But then again, why not? It seemed an alarmingly heavy commitment. But then again, I would learn a lot too. So I said yes, with some trepidation.

After an induction process telling us what to expect, what to do and not do, a selection evening put a group of potential mentors into a roomful of refugees who did the choosing. Sara selected me, and I could see why. That day, she and I happened to be the only two middle-aged women in a room filled mostly with young people: most of the refugees were young men, most of the mentors younger men and women.

Sara was a delight and an education for me, an amazingly impressive and interesting woman. She was from Somalia, not newly arrived, but had gained her refugee status some seven years earlier. She had three children in school in London, her English was quite good, but not quite good enough yet to get the kind of job she wanted. Sadly, in all that time she had made no English friend: she only knew other foreigners of various nationalities. Her children had school friends but she didn't know their parents.

Over the year we met in places she had never visited, free museums and galleries where she would return and bring her children at weekends. Sometimes in the holidays her children came too. We wandered many floors of the British Museum, the National Gallery, the London Museum, the National Portrait Gallery, Trafalgar Square, St James's Park, a trip on the London Eye to see the city from the air, a tour round the Houses of Parliament with her children and outdoor cafes on nice days.

I suspect I got more out of it than she did; as she retold her remarkable story I was enthralled. She had fought all her life, first against her father to stay at school and train as a doctor and she fought with her brothers and all those who objected to her ambition in a traditional society. And then she fought to escape with her children from war-torn horror to Kenya and on to London.

She volunteers too, stuffing envelopes for her local Labour party, but said she was too shy to speak much and make friends. I waited in suspense to hear if her oldest daughter had made it into medical school, after studying hard in their tiny two-room flat. We celebrated when her results came through, a triumph for a girl who arrived with no English, a remarkable girl now learning sign language in her spare time.

What did I offer Sara? Adult conversation, talk about politics and the world, suggestions about practical problems, struggles with the benefit system and help with English – she is hoping to pass exams for a medical post here. But above all, I think, just a connection with a London woman her age to talk about children and school and how things work.

I am left now with a sense of awe for people who arrive here with nothing after suffering war and disaster, yet make their way by sheer determination, an iron will that Sara had passed on to her children. No one meeting someone like Sara could doubt the qualities she and her children bring to this country. I learned a lot, it widened my horizons and I felt humbled by my own ease of life. But most important of all I enjoyed our meetings and I liked her company and her conversation. It is no good volunteering if it is not fun.

And somewhere in this guide there is bound to be something for everyone.

Polly Toynbee, 2007

1. Why volunteer?

It might be the adrenalin rush of manning a lifeboat off the coast of Cornwall or a quiet lunch hour teaching a child to read. It might be carrying out research into wind turbines or popping to Tesco for supplies for your housebound neighbour. It might be teaching Scouts to ski or picking up the phone at the Samaritans. In recent years the face of volunteering has undergone a transformation. Once fundraising meant trudging door to door selling raffle tickets, now it could mean skydiving out of a plane or pedalling to China. And where once volunteering overseas was a young person's activity, now retired people are packing their bags and buying a plane ticket.

Fewer people than ever might be choosing to vote in general elections. But more and more of us are taking action in our communities. It is the people's revolution, if you will. A groundswell of goodwill. 'I think historians will look back at the 21st century and quite rightly call it "the age of the volunteer",' says Justin Davis Smith of the Institute for Volunteering Research. 'There's much more recognition now of what the individual has to offer.'

In the last five years the voluntary sector has shed its fusty twinset-and-pearls image. It is no longer just for ladies who lunch. Charities have learnt that they need to be flexible to fit into potential volunteers' busy lives. And we've realised that we want something more in life than work and home. According to the latest UK government's Department for Communities and Local Government Citizenship Survey, more than three-quarters of the population of England volunteered at least once between 2004 and 2005. Some 50 per cent did so at least once a month.

This means that if you start to volunteer you will become one of almost 18 million people in England alone who are getting involved and working in groups and clubs at least once a year, and you may become one of the more than 11 million who do so at least once a month.

So, if you choose to make it an important part of your life, supporting a charity can be much more than just chipping in for the latest sponsored swim. It is about giving time as much as money. It is about getting involved locally, nationally or internationally to make a real difference to your community, your country and the wider world. And the exciting thing is that there are literally hundreds of ways to do so. We've outlined many ideas later in this book, but just to whet your appetite, you could:

- promote Greenpeace at Glastonbury music festival
- help to clean the Thames
- sit on your local Youth Justice Board

- create a community garden
- mentor a refugee from Afghanistan

Or how about:

- organising fundraising events to help disaster relief efforts
- tagging turtles in South America
- working in a school in Kenya
- helping to build a children's home in eastern Europe
- setting up a newsletter in Papua New Guinea

Some people will choose to help out in their community independently, but working with a voluntary organisation gives you the contacts, the resources and the financial backing to truly make a difference. It will also point you in the right direction if you want to use your skills overseas.

In the UK, volunteering is now a vital part of society, contributing to all areas of life. Whatever your motivation for doing it, the powerful force for change that comes with volunteering can't be underestimated. The economic value of volunteering with an organisation is said to be more than £40 billion a year. For every £1 spent on volunteering from the public purse, volunteers give £30 worth of work. In the public sector alone, if the time contributed by volunteers was evaluated it would total around £17 billion.

The government is slowly beginning to grasp the importance of volunteering, seeing it as a way of making us all a little more caring and helping to create vibrant, inclusive communities. It designated 2005 the Year of the Volunteer to raise awareness of what volunteers do. In 2006, it contributed £50 million towards the launch of **v**, a national charity that aims to recruit one million more young people into the voluntary sector in the next five years.

There are now also designated days and weeks in the year - such as the Community Service Volunteers annual Make a Difference day - to celebrate those who are involved in volunteering work and to inspire more people to give up their time for free.

Your mum survived breast cancer and you'd like to help fund research? You think refugees need more support when they arrive in Britain? You're worried about climate change? You've always fancied working abroad? The local football team needs a coach? There has never been a better time to get involved.

What's in it for me?

There is nothing wrong in considering the personal benefits of volunteering. After all, you will be investing valuable commodities - your time and your energy. The case histories threaded throughout this book show that many people have found volunteering immensely rewarding. It may sound like a cliché but it is true - volunteers report back and say that you get out what you put in. Friendships are forged, skills discovered, perceptions changed. Many have found that charity work has fundamentally changed the way they lead their lives.

Volunteering will not only give you the satisfaction of knowing you have given something back, it may also:

- improve your job prospects and employability
- give you new insights into a profession
- help you to develop new skills
- improve your confidence
- help you to meet new people and find out more about your community
- give you enjoyment

Job prospects and employability

Volunteering looks good on your CV. Giving your time to help others demonstrates to potential employers that you've got commitment, a broader outlook on life and well-developed social skills. For employers desperate for people with experience - both professional and social - volunteering could tick all the boxes and make the difference between a rejection letter and a job offer. Depending on what you choose to do, volunteering could demonstrate that you are an inspiring team leader, or someone who is self-motivated and able to work to tight deadlines. It also shows you have inter-personal skills and drive.

Volunteering can also provide you with useful business contacts that could be put to use in your existing job, or it may open the door to a new career, or a place on a college course.

Insight into a new profession

In the same way that travel has been said to broaden the mind, so volunteering can open your eyes to new possibilities. It gives you the chance to try something you might not have tried before. For example, if you spend your days working in an office, but have always thought about working with people with disabilities, volunteering in the evenings or weekends for a disability charity will give you a taste of what's involved. For some people, volunteering with vulnerable young people can persuade them to retrain to work with them full-time. Even if you're not looking to change direction, simply volunteering for your local hospice, or for a developmental organisation, or helping at the local office of a political party will broaden your outlook and perhaps offer a new appreciation of other people, or your own personal situation.

Equally, if you find out what you don't like doing, it is an invaluable exercise.

New skills

In some voluntary roles, initial training will be necessary. Some organisations will even train volunteers for formal qualifications - it is worth enquiring when you approach an organisation if this is the case. Formal training could lead to a recognised qualification, such as a National Vocational Qualification (NVQ) in the area in which you are volunteering. Some volunteering work can be used to acquire specific leadership qualifications. In sports, for example, young people from the age of 14 can obtain sports leadership awards, which can prepare them to take on a range of roles in community sports. These nationally recognised awards, offered by the British Sports Trust, give candidates the chance to develop their organisational and sporting skills, as well as learning how to set up competitions or activities.

Even without formal training, the activities you will be involved in will certainly help you to develop what are known as soft skills, such as team work, communication and leadership. If you're not a natural financier, but are chosen to be the treasurer for a local youth football team, you'll soon develop basic accountancy skills. Compiling the rota for volunteers at a charity shop will test your skills in both organisation and diplomacy.

Confidence

We've already said that volunteering can develop new skills, and sharpen a few existing ones, but just getting out there and having a go will help to improve your confidence. It is about finding your niche, and feeling supported in what you do. For some, taking a group of children with disabilities out for a day trip to the beach, or working in a pet rescue centre seems like a huge challenge, but trying it out and being successful will boost your confidence and inspire you to have another go, or try something new. The whole point of signing up to help a voluntary organisation is that you are not in it alone. You'll probably find yourself working with people who have done the job for years and will be willing to help you out. Remember too that this new-found confidence will filter into other areas of your life.

Meet new people in your community

You could walk past a building every day of the week and not know that every Friday it comes alive with the sound of music at a tea dance for older people, or that on Monday mornings it is used as a drop-in centre for single parents. Or that every Saturday morning a team of people tend to the flowerbeds in the local park or run sports activities for youngsters. Deciding to volunteer will give you a better idea of what actually goes on in your community. Not only that, unless you are volunteering from home, you will meet people of all ages, from a variety of backgrounds and with a host of experiences. You can always learn something new from people and you could also find yourself acquiring a new set of friends.

Fun

The American inventor Thomas Edison once said: 'I never did a day's work in my life. It was all fun.' And that's what volunteering should be. Enjoying what you do is as important as actually doing it.

But it is not just the work you will be doing that should be satisfying; spending time with your fellow volunteers should also be enjoyable. Volunteering is a bonding experience, whether you are working in an orphanage in India or the wetlands of Hertfordshire.

KATH BANNISTER, 48 'The experience of being a volunteer has never left me – it also helped me get a new job.'

The unpaid work that I did when I was a mother with two small children helped me to get the job I have now and the skills I've picked up over the years. Organising groups of people, running committees, looking for funding, building up networks, building up contacts – all feed into what I do now.

I did a lot when my children were babies and toddlers. I'd moved to the other side of the country and I didn't want to be isolated as a newcomer and a new mother. I gradually got involved in the neighbourhood – in the local community centre giving people benefits advice, on the residents' association for my estate, at the nearby playgroup.

I never saw it as a means to get a job. That wasn't on the agenda. However I was told about a vacancy for maternity leave for a local community worker and someone suggested I apply. I got the job and have worked in the same sort of area ever since. I'm now employed by the district council on community regeneration projects. In a way I was doing the same work as a volunteer but I just didn't realise it.

A big part of my job is encouraging people to volunteer. My advice to them is to go in with an open mind, look around locally and don't expect people to say how fantastic you are – often they can be quite antagonistic! Try something you think you might like but use it to explore what you want both professionally and personally. Sometimes it is as useful to discover what you don't like doing as what you do.

The experience of being a volunteer has never left me and has meant that I've been able to bring a deeper understanding to my work. If you've never volunteered you don't know what it's like. I try not to make unnecessary demands on people, the fact that they're not being paid is always on my mind. In another way I still look back on my volunteer days with great fondness. As a volunteer you can say what you want. I remember when we demonstrated against a dangerous stretch of road by forming a human chain across it. It was amazing and it really proved a point and it persuaded the council to act. It is not something I could do now. One can still agitate but it must be done behind the scenes.

AILEEN JONES, 43, winner of an RNLI bronze medal for gallantry 'I always say to people, "I can drive a boat but I can't cook!"'

It was 11.15 a.m. on a Tuesday morning in August 2004. My pager went off and I hurried down to the RNLI's lifeboat station. A fisherman was stranded in his boat on the Nash Banks – part of the most dangerous stretch of coastline in Britain – and

because I was the first qualified crew member to arrive it was my job to lead the team to rescue him.

I remember coming around the sandbanks in our boat and thinking 'God, we'll not get through this to him.' It was just too rough. The waves were four metres high. He had no engine. His anchors wouldn't hold. He was at the mercy of the water.

But I wasn't frightened. You can't be when you're on a shout. You just have to get on with the job and let the adrenalin get you through. You haven't got time to think about it. You have to work as a team.

In the end it took three and a half hours to rescue him. Afterwards, I knew we had done a good job but I didn't get emotional about it. If you get scared then you're not the right person to do this kind of volunteer work. I always say to people – 'I can drive a boat but I can't cook!'

The sea has always been a huge part of my life. I used to go out in my dad's boat when I was growing up. When I was seven I spotted a boat firing distress flares off the seafront and ran down to the RNLI to tell them. it is just something I always wanted to do.

However, I couldn't volunteer until I was 17 and then, like everyone, I had to do a lot of training before I could go out on the boat. You start off as a shore helper and gradually work your way through the lifeboat college in Poole. I became an actual crew member when I was 32.

In the early days it was a very male-dominated world and it was difficult to break in. They had never had a woman in this station before. But gradually things have changed. Women are much more accepted now. I'm just part of the crew.

Some people think it is glamorous but it is not. You have to go out in horrible weather. There are a lot of dirty jobs involved. Sometimes it is freezing. You've really got to want to do it. You have to muck in with the boys and get on with it. But the camaraderie is amazing and it is a wonderful feeling to know that you can save people's lives.

NICK, 52* 'Being a Samaritan has taught me to be more compassionate.'

I've been aware of the Samaritans for many years, not least because it is a service I used myself when I was younger. I've always been curious how a stranger on the telephone can actually help someone and how listening to someone in a non-judgemental way and allowing them to speak can benefit them. I suppose I always wondered if I could do it.

I believe that there's nothing that can't be talked about, and that talking really helps people, but often it is impossible to speak to those who are closest to you. It is easier to confide in someone who is completely anonymous and when it is confidential.

Sometimes callers come on the line and say they have done awful things. You don't know whether it is true or not but it doesn't matter. No calls can be traced. We can't call the police. We can't even call an ambulance unless they make it absolutely clear that they want us to. The key is confidentiality.

Absolutely anything can happen on a shift and that's why I keep doing it. When the phone goes you have two rings to compose yourself before you pick it up and after that there's no knowing what the person will say. There is no typical call. Calls can come from anywhere in the country. You could be talking to someone from Glasgow or from the next town.

I work about 15 hours a month for the Samaritans, including one overnight shift. It still surprises me that I can listen to people talking about really dreadful things that have happened to them in their lives and not get sucked into their drama or brought down by it. That's partly to do with the training and the way we are taught to listen and partly to do with the support system around us. Everyone has a mentor and a minder and each shift has a leader who you can talk to.

Over the two years that I've been doing it I've developed my listening skills and acquired an ability to listen without making judgement. I don't feel as if I've got to jump in and solve the problem. It has extended my understanding of people and I think it has made me more compassionate.

It has been a privilege. In the most successful calls I have a sense of having helped. Someone might ring and be incoherent at the beginning. They might be crying so much they can barely speak. If during the phone call I can hear their breathing calm down and they gradually feel able to articulate some of what they feel then I have helped in some way. Sometimes something awful will have just happened. Sometimes it is the tiniest thing. They might have walked past someone who reminds them of their mother who died 15 years ago and it opens something up. It can be anything and everything.

Applicants go through an intensive selection day where they are observed, both in interviews and groups. If they're successful they go through to a training programme. Even when they start taking calls it still takes from nine months to a year before they're properly qualified. You need to think carefully about why you want to do it. Be clear about your commitment. And then give it a try. I've seen the most improbable people be absolutely brilliant at it.

It is a unique service in a way – absolutely non-judgemental, non-denominational. It is about the caller being able to talk about anything. It is about giving people as much space and time as they need. For some of the people who call it is about being valued for who they are for the first time in their lives.

* For reasons of confidentiality Nick cannot reveal his personal details.

2 Who volunteers?

There is no one single type of volunteer. The joy of volunteering is that anyone, whatever their circumstances, can get involved. Everyone has something to offer - whether it is answering the phone at a local hospice, offering free legal advice to someone with financial problems, digging up weeds in the local park, taking a group of young people to a theme park, or simply using their cheerfulness and energy to brighten up a lunch club for the elderly.

Volunteers come from all walks of life and they represent all ages and demographics - you only have to look at the person with a collecting tin outside a station, or someone working in a charity shop, or a coach training a football team to see this diversity in action. In fact, charities need a diverse range of people on board in order to be successful, both in getting the work done and in attracting others to the cause. Diversity means organisations can offer vastly different skills and services - from accountants who sit on a committee to grandparents who go into school to help children learn to read. All volunteers are valuable, whether they are students looking for work experience; retired professionals looking to fill the extra time they now have; people out of work trying to re-enter the job market; or busy professionals who want to make a meaningful contribution to society.

Whether in full-time work or not, there are a few categories of volunteers for whom there are certain considerations. This chapter will address these issues.

Young people

It is never too early to start volunteering and it can offer you a wealth of experience.

The phrase 'learning by doing' is what it is all about, particularly for young people. This means getting involved with your local community, whether that's through helping to run a children's club, serving dinner at a homeless shelter or giving out leaflets for a local charity in your town centre. All this will help you develop the 'soft skills' that employers love - communication, teamwork, confidence, leadership, time management.

If you start volunteering, you won't be alone. According to the government's statistics survey, 29 per cent of 16 to 24-year-olds volunteered through a group or club at least once a month in the 12 months prior to responding to a Citizenship Survey in 2005. That figure rose to 47 per cent for young people who carried out volunteering on their own.

Fitting volunteering in around your school, college or university work may not be easy. If you need to travel to and from a venue or event you could find the hours you can volunteer limited by when your parents can drive you, or by public transport timetables. But having a go will put your job application or university admission form head and shoulders above those who spent their evenings and weekends slouched in front of the television. For young people aged 18 and older, taking a gap year before starting your degree offers a great opportunity to take up longer-term voluntary work in the UK or overseas.

Businesses value volunteering experience very highly. Companies often say it can be the deciding factor between candidates. A survey carried out by Reed Executive of more than 200 of the UK's top businesses found that almost three-quarters preferred to recruit candidates with volunteering experience listed on their CVs. And university admissions officers judging between two students with the same predicted grades will inevitably look at how that candidate spent their time away from their books. And in the future, volunteering might even help towards the cost of university. The government recently indicated that it was considering reducing tuition fees for volunteering students.

Volunteering is also a good way to explore new areas of interest that could affect future career choices. If you've always harboured ideas of working in medicine or healthcare, regular volunteering at a local hospice or for an elderly people's home will give you a practical idea of what to expect. On the other hand, volunteering could completely change your career goals. A stint on the local hospital radio could open your eyes to a career in the media, instead of the one you were thinking of pursuing in, say, the legal profession.

Organisations are actively being encouraged to create better, more meaningful volunteering opportunities for young people, particularly those under 18. They are also trying to be flexible, so you can fit the work around studies or paid employment, and offering incentives, such as travel expenses and a good reference.

The charity **v** was set up in 2006 to look specifically at how more 16 to 25-year-olds can get involved in volunteering, and how to ensure there are plenty of opportunities open to them. **v** is a youth-led organisation, and has an advisory board made up of 20 young people. Look at their website www.wearev.com for possible grant opportunities.

Of course, there's nothing to stop you starting your own project. You may be able to get funding to do so. The Government has two new funds for young people: the Youth Opportunity Fund (YOF) and the Youth Capital Fund (YCF). The Youth Opportunity Fund provides money for projects and activities in your area, while funding from the Youth Capital Fund can be used to buy the premises and equipment needed to get activities going. Contact your local authority (www.upmystreet.com) for more information.

Many funding organisations are now keen to offer finance. Youthbank (www.youthbank.org.uk) is managed and promoted locally by young people and offers up to £750 a term. The Big Boost also gives awards to young people (between ages 11-25) ranging from £250 to £5000, to help them get their ideas off the ground. Visit www.thebigboost.org.uk to find out if you are eligible and see what other people have already done. To find out more about setting up your own project, see page 71.

ALEC FOULKES is a 15-year-old high-school pupil in Birmingham. He volunteers with Get Hooked on Fishing scheme.

I got involved in Get Hooked ages ago. I was asked if I wanted to become a coach, and I've been doing that for two to three years. I coach people from all over the area.

The reason I got involved is because I've been fishing since I was a child and I wanted to pass on my knowledge and get new people into it. It is really hard to get into, especially if you're a kid, because there's so much expensive equipment that's hard to get, which we can provide.

I don't get paid, or get any expenses, I do it for free. In the summer, during the holidays, I can coach two to three times a week, but if it's not a holiday I go every other Saturday. I'm happy to fit it around my schoolwork, because each session lasts only about four hours and starts early in the morning.

Before I was fishing with Get Hooked, I was really nervous talking to people, but it has improved my confidence. Hopefully it will help me to get into college to do fishery management.

Retired people

While some people may have been volunteering all their lives, the free time that comes with not having regular work commitments could inspire you to volunteer for the first time. If you've spent your working life behind a desk in an office dreaming of establishing a dance school for children, you'll now have the time to investigate the possibilities. You might always have had a love of the arts and a passion for educating young people, so now could be the right time to become an education officer at your local heritage site.

If you have spent a large part of your career in management or business, then the knowledge you've gained over the years could make you the ideal candidate for a trusteeship. Charity trustees make up the management board of an organisation and have the ultimate responsibility for it, so this will be perfect for someone who is level-headed and knows how to manage responsibilities. Read more on becoming a trustee on page 52.

The charity Age Concern is specifically encouraging older people to get involved in local crime policy and prevention, through volunteering in the criminal justice system, in a local neighbourhood watch scheme or on a crime partnership panel.

But you don't have to stay in the UK. Retirement can open volunteering doors around the world. The development charity VSO, for example, is particularly keen to recruit older volunteers - people who have the practical skills and experience that come with age – to help to train others and support communities in poorer communities.

While the huge benefits that age and experience can bring to volunteering are starting to be recognised by organisations and the government, some organisations will have their own retirement age for volunteers. This can depend on the type of volunteering. For example, some charities are not keen on using people over the age of 65 as drivers or first aiders, but are happy for those helping with administration to carry on indefinitely.

Although organisations claim they have problems getting employer's liability insurance cover for people over the age of 65, particularly for driving, this needn't stop you from getting involved. Find out more about volunteering and the law in Chapter seven, page 85.

At present, only 27 per cent of people aged 65 and over take part in community and voluntary activities. The number drops further for the over-75s. But with people living longer, in ten years' time half of the UK's population will be over 50, which means your skills are soon going to become highly sought after if organisations do not want to find themselves with a recruitment crisis.

52-year-old HARRY STOYLES, from West Yorkshire, is retired. He volunteers with Surviving Trauma After Rape (STAR).

I'm one of STAR's support workers, which involves meeting men and women, and in some cases children and adolescents, who have been raped or seriously sexually assaulted. We provide emotional and practical support, such as contacting the police on their behalf or accompanying them when they go to court. I'm also a victim support volunteer and part of that training was taking over where support workers left off. I also worked for an organisation that supports women whose children have been sexually abused.

For six years I have been working in the area around sexual abuse and sexual assault.

You see people in a raw state, often not many hours or days after a rape or assault. My task is to deal with their trauma, try to help them to come to terms with it. It can be daunting and very emotional at times. The victim can tell you as much or as little as they want. For some it is cathartic. Others can't face talking about it as they also have to go through the process with the police in minute detail.

Hours can vary. When I first started doing it, it was about five or six hours a week, but now I'm not seeing as many people, so it is probably about a couple of hours a week. There are two or three other male volunteers, but I'm certainly the longest-serving man there.

Being male in an environment where 90 per cent of perpetrators are men can be quite tough. But you come away feeling you are beginning to help someone put their

life back together. I also feel as though I have helped redress the balance. I like to think what I'm doing is providing a role model – I'm showing them that not all men are evil.

Refugees and asylum seekers

People with refugee status (or those who have exceptional leave to remain) can do any type of work including volunteering. Although the law dictates that asylum seekers are not allowed to undertake paid or unpaid work, if you have refugee status you are allowed to volunteer and claim out-of-pocket expenses without breaking the law. If you are in the process of appealing against a decision not to award you refugee status, you can still carry on volunteering.

The distinction between volunteering and unpaid work depends on the type of business or organisation you are involved with. The Home Office defines unpaid employment as helping out in a private business, perhaps on behalf of a relative, in return for a non-monetary benefit, such as accommodation or food. But if you work for a charity, a body that raises money for charity, or a voluntary organisation, then the work you do will be legally classed as volunteering.

If you volunteer while you are an asylum seeker you could be in a better position to get work if your claim is accepted and volunteering for an organisation in an area of interest could offer you training, practical experience and the chance to network.

We live in a multicultural society, and with that diversity comes a variety of specific needs; volunteering with other asylum seeks could be one of the ways in which your experience might be particularly valuable. Who better to understand what help a newly arrived asylum seeker needs than someone who might have been in a similar position?

SABA WYATT, 42, is a refugee from Ethiopia. A part-time administration assistant, she is setting up a local Ethiopian community group in Coventry.

It was very hard for me when I first arrived in Britain from Ethiopia back in 1990. I was 25 years old and I'd left my whole family behind – mother, father, sister. I was running away from a government that was hunting down people like me. The authorities frowned upon anyone who wanted to get an education and my friends were being killed.

London seemed alien in the beginning. But in a way I was lucky. Because I had worked with foreigners in Ethiopia I knew how to mix, how to get on with people. Gradually everyone started to know who I was and Britain began to feel like home.

It is not as easy for everyone. If they don't know how to socialise they can soon become isolated. They worry about being deported. They're anxious about their families. I've known people get depressed, even some who have committed suicide because they have no one to talk to who understands them.

So now I'm in the process of setting up a community group of Ethiopians near where I live in Coventry. Initially a few of us started to hook up through the internet but now we've realised that there are lots of us near here. It is a revelation.

This is just the beginning – we're trying to write the constitution, decide what we stand for. Once we've got all the groundwork done we can start applying for funds. Part of my motivation is to tell people what Ethiopia is really like. Strangers used to say to me: 'You can't be Ethiopian because you're not skinny enough.' People just think about famine and Bob Geldof but in fact we have a lot of history. I want to overthrow some of the stereotypes.

All my spare time is taken up with trying to organise everything. But it is difficult sometimes. Ethiopians come from different tribes and bringing them together is very hard. I just keep reminding myself that if we're non-political and non-religious, there will be a way. I really agree with Tony Blair – the more people know about us the more we can integrate. Cultures need to mix with one another. There should be a two-way street – the more we educate people about our culture, the more accepted we will be.

Job seekers

Volunteering while you are out of work could dramatically help in your search for a job. It could also be a stepping stone back into society if you haven't been able to work due to illness or injury.

Receiving welfare benefits is no bar to volunteering – you can get involved in voluntary work and still claim jobseeker's allowance. For the purpose of benefit payments, the government defines volunteering as unpaid work for a not-for-profit organisation, for which the volunteer receives no more than out-of-pocket expenses, such as for travel and meal costs and for any specialised equipment needed for the work.

Before undertaking any voluntary work, always notify your local benefits office so that they are aware of what you are doing and agree that what you intend to do is suitable. Some benefits offices have been known to stop benefits if they have not been told in advance that a claimant is taking up volunteering.

People with disabilities

If you have a disability, volunteering should not affect your right to receive disability living allowance.

Volunteers are not afforded the same legal rights as paid workers when it comes to discrimination issues (see page 83 for further information on volunteering and the law). Any good organisation, though, should apply the same rules on diversity for volunteers as they do for paid staff. And all organisations are encouraged to have an equal opportunities policy in place, which you should ask to see if you feel you have been unfairly treated.

Transport arrangements have been found to be one of the biggest barriers to volunteering for people with physical disabilities. If this is something that concerns you, ask the organisation for which you want to volunteer if they can help to organise transport for you. If you have to arrange your own, you should be reimbursed for expenses. Ask also about whether the building you may find yourself in has wheelchair access if that is relevant (it might be worth mentioning to the organisation that the Centre for Accessible Environments can advise it on how to create a more wheelchair-friendly building).

If your disability is not physical, it is up to you whether you disclose it. If you do, the organisation may be better placed to offer support. For example, if you need to take medication that could make you tired, the people you are volunteering with will be able to arrange for you to take more breaks.

It might be worth visiting a local volunteering centre for advice on choosing the right sort of voluntary opportunity for you. Some centres run support programmes for people with disabilities, and may even attend an interview with you.

Benefits and volunteering at a glance

Jobseeker's allowance: claimants are fully entitled to volunteer as long as they remain available for and are actively seeking work. There is no limit on the number of hours, but it is likely that someone volunteering full time may be regarded as not having time to actively seek work. Job seekers are also entitled to 48 hours' notice if asked to attend an interview and a week's notice before starting work.

Income support: claimants can volunteer for as many hours as they like.

Incapacity benefit/disability living allowance: claimants are fully entitled to volunteer and this should not call into question a person's fitness to work. There is no limit on the number of hours spent volunteering. Be aware that the government is expected to make changes to incapacity benefit in the near future, which could affect these claims.

DAVID CREW, 38, has epilepsy and Asperger's syndrome. He volunteers for the RSPB at Rye Meads nature reserve in Hertfordshire.

I chose the RSPB because I like outdoor work and had spent several months in my house not really mixing with other people. I thought this would be a good opportunity to get outdoors and enjoy some physically demanding work while meeting like-minded – and hopefully not judgemental – people. I am not really a birder and do struggle with names and calls from time to time, but since I joined the RSPB as a volunteer I have greatly improved.

Tasks like digging holes are a real source of stress relief and act as therapy and a way of letting off some steam. I can also feel myself getting fitter and stronger and this all adds to my confidence.

It took all my efforts to approach the RSPB and introduce myself to the warden. I didn't feel any hostility or wariness regarding my condition, and I was immediately offered two work roles, on a Tuesday and Thursday.

There are some tasks which I can't get involved with, such as ladder work and machinery, and I will never be able to drive as I couldn't handle it, but I am hardly faced with any restrictions and know that the work I do is appreciated. We constantly get praise when we complete a job and this goes a long way.

I enjoy lending my time to worthy causes and find that doing so gets me out and about and back into society.

Ex-offenders

According to the Chartered Institute of Personnel and Development, about 20 per cent of the working population have a criminal record, often for minor offences, so ex-offenders represent a significant group of people with a wealth of skills and experience.

If you have recently left prison, volunteering could be the vital route into employment, as it could help you to update skills, or use any new ones developed while in prison through education and training programmes. Just as importantly, volunteering could give you the confidence to apply for jobs and give you someone to put down as a referee on your CV.

The crime reduction charity Nacro receives thousands of phone calls to its resettlement helpline from people wanting to know what information they need to supply when applying for paid or voluntary work. The organisation says many ex-offenders are put off applying because they worry what reaction they will get from potential co-workers if they disclose their past.

In certain circumstances a criminal record can stop you doing certain things: for example, if you have been convicted of a drink-driving offence you might not be eligible for work that involves transporting people. It is worth asking the organisation for which you want to volunteer whether they have a written policy on the involvement of ex-offenders. This should give you some idea of whether you are likely to be accepted as a volunteer. Under the Rehabilitation of Offenders Act, spent convictions should not be taken into account by an organisation for most paid or unpaid positions, so ex-offenders are not required to disclose them. Most offences become spent after five years, but convictions that lead to conditional discharges normally become spent after one year.

The exception is for work involving children or vulnerable adults. Anyone convicted of crimes against children is automatically banned, by law, from working with anyone under the age of 18, or with vulnerable adults. For those with other convictions who want to work with these groups, all offences (regardless of whether or not they are spent), cautions, reprimands or final warnings must be disclosed to the voluntary organisation. You will be subject to police checks (see Volunteering and the law on page 85), but unless your convictions relate to violent, sexual or drug offences, don't assume you will automatically be barred from working with these groups.

Many organisations already require potential volunteers to have an interview or an informal chat, and perhaps provide references, before they begin work. The likelihood of this happening is probably increased for ex-offenders, so be prepared.

Finally, your involvement in volunteering is an equal opportunity issue. Although volunteers aren't covered by employment law, organisations should have an equal opportunities policy, which any good charity should apply to both paid staff and volunteers. If such a policy exists you will have reason to complain to someone in the organisation, if not to any legal authority, if you feel you have been treated unfairly because of your criminal record.

3. Deciding what to do

So, you know that you want to volunteer. The next step is to decide what type of volunteering to do. With more than six million non-governmental organisations (NGOs) and not-for-profit organisations worldwide involved in an array of social and environmental work, selecting something might seem overwhelming. Everyone will find that their skills are in demand by a variety of different organisations, so the trick will be deciding what really motivates you.

What matters to you?

No one is going to heave themselves out of bed in the morning without being paid if they're not passionate about what they're volunteering for. You need to choose something that matters to you. It might be a good cause which has touched you personally. It might be sport, or looking after animals, or going out and spending time with people. For others it is fighting to eradicate poverty, or promoting penal reform. Think of ways you can translate these interests into volunteering. If you like sport, why not help at the local youth football team? If you love animals, think about helping at the local pet rescue centre. And if you like helping people, how about signing up with the St John Ambulance?

For some people, an illness experienced by a close relative or friend can be enough to spur them to start volunteering for a charity, either as a way of expressing gratitude for the help it offered in that time of need or simply in memory of a loved one.

If you can't immediately translate your main interests into a volunteering opportunity, try thinking about what you would want to change, create or fix in your community or wider society if you were given the money and the permission to do so.

What do you enjoy?

Volunteering works best if you feel happy with your contribution. So think about the environment in which you want to volunteer. If you are stuck in an office all day, would you be happy to man phones at a call centre at the weekend, or would you prefer to do something completely different, maybe something that indulges a hobby? If you work with children throughout the week, perhaps you would want use your skills and experience to help run a youth group. Or would working with adults come as a huge relief?

Discovering what you want to do could mean thinking about what you *don't* want to do. If you do get involved in volunteering work that doesn't feel right, or doesn't inspire you, for whatever reason, then don't do it.

If you find yourself in this situation it is worth speaking to someone in charge, perhaps an immediate supervisor, before moving on in case there are other opportunities within the organisation that are better suited to you.

What do you want to achieve?

Think specifically about what you want to achieve through volunteering.

- Would you like to contribute to your community?
- Do you want to meet new people?
- Do you want to receive practical training and experience that could help you get a job or a promotion?

If you are hoping to widen your circle of friends, look for an opportunity that makes you part of a team, such as working with a youth group, or for your local environmental group. If you have a more global outlook, then think about which campaigning group addresses the issues that concern and interest you. Think also about where you want to volunteer - do you want to work in your home town or venture further afield?

There is no doubt that volunteering will look good on your CV, but do you want to get practical training and experience that could help you get a job? Look out for any opportunities related to the kind of work you might like to do. For example, if you already have some IT skills, perhaps you could learn to develop web pages for a charity.

What are you good at?

The next thing to consider is what specific skills you can offer an organisation. Are you a practical 'hands-on' person, or better at strategic planning and management? Can you speak a language, cut hair, do accounts, drive a minibus? Perhaps you've been told that you are a good listener or a great motivator. Or maybe your ability to negotiate is a strength. Perhaps you have a specialist skill to offer, such as medical or legal, that could be put to good use. Once you have defined your skills, organisations such as TimeBank or local volunteering centres can then try to match them up with the requirements of local or national schemes.

Whatever it is you are good at, there is bound to be an organisation that is waiting to snap you up. Although there will be some opportunities that require specialist training or technical knowledge, such as flying a rescue helicopter or sailing a lifeboat, many will offer voluntary work that can be carried out by the majority of people. In volunteering there is no such thing as 'unskilled'. There are only skills waiting to be developed.

How much responsibility do you want?

You can have as little or as much as you want. Think about what you are comfortable doing. Are you happy being in charge, or would you prefer to be just part of the team?

Do you want to help a charity organise a big event in the local community centre, or are you happier collecting money in the high street? Remember, you won't be on your own. Volunteering could give you the security to test out your leadership skills.

How much time can you give?

This is a crucial question, so be honest with yourself and with the organisation for which you want to volunteer. If you are pulled in different directions by family or work commitments, it is important to establish how much time you can realistically spare in advance. So think carefully about all the things you already do in any one week or month. It might be helpful to write down which hours or days are usually free. It may be better to start volunteering for a few hours a week or month and build up from there, or even just try a one-off project. Don't make long-term commitment unless you are absolutely sure you can fit them around your work or family obligations. Think also about the best times to volunteer. Do you work or study in the mornings, so that you are able to fit in voluntary work in the afternoons? If you work long hours during the week, volunteering in the evenings might prove tricky, so think about having a go at the weekend.

You might want to choose a position that will teach you new skills that could prove useful in other areas of your life, such as at work or in your favourite sport. If you have a family, choose a volunteering project in which they can all participate and have fun, such as some form of environmental work in a local park.

The good news is that the new climate of volunteering means an opportunity can usually be fitted in somehow. Businesses are starting to sit up and take notice, encouraging employee schemes that can be run doing the working day, and there are more 'virtual' opportunities (see Chapter four: Striking a balance, page 63). Many volunteering projects are designed with flexibility in mind. Most not-for-profit organisations don't keep nine-to-five hours. Instead they will, as much as they can, operate according to the needs of their volunteers, organising evening meetings, weekend training or early morning interviews.

I volunteer once a fortnight

MARY O'DONNELL, 31, is a civil servant. She volunteers on her local Youth Justice Board in London.

Last year I started to worry that I was living in a bubble – that I could go through my life never really understanding what other people's communities are like. At the same time the whole issue of young people and crime is something I've been obsessed about for ages. The Youth Justice Board has been a chance for me to do something proactive rather than sitting back and doing nothing.

The scheme involves six days of training. It meets once a fortnight. It is for young people who have pleaded guilty to a crime at their first appearance in court and it

is a chance for them to repair some of the harm they've done, to understand the link between the crime and the community. The panel talks to them about why they've offended and what it would take for them not to do it again. For many it is the first time that they've been offered the chance to do something constructive.

We're a small part of what is going on in their world but the hope is that it gives them an opportunity to turn their lives around before it is too late. It is about restorative justice rather than straightforward punishment. The whole experience has helped me to see the world in a less black-and-white way. It is also given me a way of connecting with the community I live in. I don't come from London. Before I did this I had my job, my friends, but no real roots here. It is helped me to build a relationship with the city. I've realised, what's the point of living here if you only see the same kind of people all the time?

I volunteer one day a week

MARGARET ROGERS, retired, volunteers for the Meningitis Trust

When my granddaughter, Lauren, was six weeks old she contracted pneumococcal meningitis. She went to hospital, but was turned away twice. The third time there was a different doctor, by which time she had started to fit. That doctor called an ambulance and they took her to hospital in Bath, where she spent the next three weeks. They had to resuscitate her. She's still got all her limbs, but she has some disabilities. She's partially deaf, has speech difficulties and mobility problems, but at least she's still here.

While she was in hospital I phoned the Meningitis Trust. They have been very good to my daughter, supplying Lauren with a special bike, and they are paying for her to have speech therapy during the school holidays.

It was very difficult watching my daughter when she was in hospital, and standing there with my grandson, who was three, and him asking why mummy and daddy were crying. I had to be strong for them. But once Lauren started school I felt at a loss and suffered severe depression. I put in so much keeping everyone else together I hadn't thought about me. I've been having counselling with the trust for the past six months and feel 99 per cent better. Because of this and how good they were to Lauren I have been going weekly to the trust and doing any administrative jobs they want me to do, because I feel I must put something back.

With the counselling, the trust was really on the ball. I think they understood me because they know the side effects. I found it much easier to talk to them than to my own doctor. They were really able to help.

Meningitis is an illness for which you are racing against time. Some charities deal with patients who have had time to adjust, but with meningitis you are up against it. There have been cases where children with the illness have gone to bed and not woken up. It is devastating. I feel that I would like to get out there and make people aware of the disease. If there was a women's group who wanted someone to tell them about my experiences, I would be there. I don't think I could do counselling or work on the helpline, but I would like to get on my soapbox.

I volunteered for six weeks

CAROLINE GOSNEY, 19, is a student. She volunteered for a six-week expedition in Madagascar with an environmental group.

I had never scuba-dived before in my life - and I had certainly never studied marine biology - but soon after arriving in Madagascar I was swimming among schools of fluorescent-coloured fish, monitoring octopus populations and exploring underwater caves and coral reefs no one had ever seen before.

I first decided to travel to Andavadoaka, a tiny village of just 1,200 people on the south-western coast of Madagascar, to have a unique holiday and see the world. But by the end of my six-week adventure, I felt I had done a lot more than just see the world. I felt I had helped improve it.

The journey was led by the London-based Blue Ventures, a non-profit organisation that coordinates expeditions aimed at promoting the health of marine areas.

My team arrived in Andavadoaka after a 22-hour ride on a boutre, a wooden sailing boat with no engine or toilet. The long journey, however, was made worthwhile when we were joined by humpback whales breaching close to the boat.

Our days in Andavadoaka began early - about 5.30 a.m. - and we were dressed in rubber wetsuits and motoring out to sea just as the sun began to peek over the horizon. We were often greeted on these morning outings by dolphins, turtles, sharks, manta rays or flying fish jumping from the water.

Once at the dive site, we began conducting surveys of marine life. We laid a 20-metre tape on the ocean floor - not an easy task with the underwater currents - and then waited for exotic fish to congregate so we could measure their populations. I had never before imagined myself sitting on the bottom of the ocean watching a Clown Trigger fish with its bright yellow lips and pink fins.

Our first few weeks in Andavadoaka were spent being trained in diving, ecology and the identification of marine species. The data collected during our daily ocean surveys were used to develop management plans with local villagers that will ensure the fish, octopus and other ocean resources they rely upon for survival are not depleted by over-fishing or threatened by growing commercial activities.

The local villagers recently established a new marine reserve based on our data - a very satisfying outcome.

How much time will it take?

Once you have decided how much time you can spare, you need to have some idea of the demands different activities may make on that time. The following list should help by showing the number of minutes per week you might spend on each activity.

20 minutes

- Help an older person to get out and about again by giving them a lift to a lunch club
- Use your vote, write a letter to your local MP on an issue that matters to you

40 minutes

- Boost your CV and make a real difference by becoming a trustee of a charity

45 minutes

- Help charity shops to maximise their sales profits by window dressing or customising second-hand clothing
- Join a local carnival and start making floats and costumes for next summer's events
- Help yourself and others by setting up a weight-loss support group

60 minutes

- Appeal to local celebrities and help to organise fundraising events
- Help a child to learn to read by reading in schools
- Offer support to survivors of domestic violence by becoming a volunteer counsellor
- Support a group of teenagers running their own projects to improve their local community or environment
- If you think everybody needs good neighbours you could be a neighbour dispute mediator and help communities to resolve local clashes

90 minutes

- Help kids to put together productions by giving time at a children's theatre
- Coach a sports team, from football to volleyball
- Become a tour guide at a stately home or other national heritage site
- Become a beach watcher and clean up beaches and undertake surveys of the coastal landscape

100 minutes

- Use your time to change someone's life for the better by becoming a mentor for a young person in care

120 minutes

- Budding superstar DJs can get a foot on the showbiz ladder by presenting on hospital or community radio
- Help elderly people to take care of their pets by walking them, taking them to the vet or even 'fostering' them if the owner has to go into hospital

180 minutes

- Join a 'green gym'. Environmental volunteers get fresh air, and better bodies, by clearing woodland, stone-walling or planting hedges

200 minutes

- Bring out the Jamie Oliver in yourself and get cooking at a homeless shelter

360 minutes

- Save lives at sea by becoming a lifeboat crew member

4. Volunteering opportunities

There are thousands of opportunities available for would-be volunteers both in the UK and abroad. This chapter highlights a number of sectors that commonly use volunteers.

Advocacy

If you want to speak up and support those in society whose voices are rarely heard or often ignored, then advocacy volunteering might be right for you.

You could find yourself involved in helping young adults with disabilities to make informed choices about their lives, and giving them the confidence to let their wishes be known and understood. Perhaps you will be helping older people to solve problems about where they should live or how to manage their finances, or supporting refugees or asylum seekers when faced with housing and employment problems or prejudice. Or you could arrange social outings to build confidence among a group of people with learning difficulties, perhaps to the cinema or the shopping centre.

You will probably be required to undergo some training before volunteering in this area, and good communication and listening skills, and a caring, non-judgemental attitude are essential. Specific knowledge of finance, housing or health services will be a bonus.

While many organisations will have voluntary openings for advocacy work within their specific fields, there are some groups that focus solely on this area. Advocacy Partners, for example, works with people with learning, physical and sensory disabilities, older people and those with mental health needs around London and Surrey (see page 91). Part of its work has involved helping older people to continue living in their own homes by offering support and helping them to adapt their houses.

Animals and wildlife

Animal lovers should find a variety of voluntary opportunities, from office work, fundraising and staffing shops, to helping in rescue centres and shelters, fostering abandoned pets, walking dogs from a dogs' home or spending a few hours a month as a volunteer guide at your local zoo or wildlife park. If you enjoy fishing you could use your hobby to monitor and improve fish habitats, or help to teach others how to fish.

Organisations that are always looking for volunteers include the veterinary charity PDSA, which helps sick and injured animals, the RSPCA and the RSPB. The Blue Cross, which re-homes unwanted or abandoned animals and helps people on low incomes with vet's bills, also has a children's educational programme and a helpline for owners whose pets have died, for which it needs volunteers.

Dog and cat owners could offer the use of their pets as a medical aid through the charity Pets As Therapy. The organisation arranges for volunteers and their good-natured animals to make therapeutic visits to hospitals, hospices, nursing and care homes and special needs schools. Some children and adults who find it difficult to communicate with other people have been known to open up when they have regular contact with a dog or cat. Other schemes offer owners the chance to take their animals into schools to help to educate children on how to look after their pets.

Organisations concerned with animals not indigenous to the UK, such as rhinos or mountain gorillas, also need volunteers to help to raise the profile of the charity in the UK, to assist with administration work and to get involved in fundraising.

The Wildlife Trusts organisation is also a good source of voluntary work. It has 47 local trusts around the UK, working with local communities to protect wildlife habitats. Volunteers can get involved in outdoor tasks or use their IT or financial skills in the office. There are also opportunities to join societies that work to promote the amenities in local parks. This could include monitoring and maintaining the quality of the trees and flowers, improving the landscape, supporting guided walks and other activities and ensuring that local people know about what goes on in the park.

KATHRYN SALOMON, from north-west London, is retired. She volunteers for Blue Cross and Pets As Therapy.

I volunteer for Pets As Therapy (PAT) and I take my greyhound, Gracie, once a month to Edgware community hospital and a psychiatric ward for teenagers. Gracie was a rescue dog who we adopted after her racing days ended. I just sit – it is the dog that's the most important thing. People come along to sit with Gracie and spend an hour just stroking her. It makes them feel better. In fact it is been medically proven that animals can improve people's physical and mental well-being.

I spend more time now working on the children's education programme for the Blue Cross. We do assemblies and class visits. We're not just talking about dogs. In assemblies we could be talking about the needs of our pets, or in class visits, for young children, how to stay safe with animals. I call it how to love our pets and how to stay safe with them.

I do class sessions and for the last quarter of an hour children can come up and stroke the dog. The dog has to pass a temperament test to be able to do it.

Apart from pet responsibility, so many children are frightened of dogs, for all sorts of reasons, and meeting Gracie is often the first time they stroke one. Some say they won't touch her, but when they see their classmates stroking her, they do. It is a huge step forward for them.

I do enjoy working with children. It is very rewarding. I have had letters saying 'I will look after my cat better', and it is a huge thing if children are not frightened by

animals any more. If they are scared they might be too frightened to go into a park or walk along a road. The fear can affect your whole life.

Arts and leisure

A great way of putting your hobby to good use is volunteering in the arts. From inspiring children to draw to helping to run a short film, there is a wealth of volunteering opportunities that could inspire those interested in the arts.

A first port of call should be the Voluntary Arts Network, which can provide advice and contact details in all areas of the arts. It doesn't arrange placements, but its website, www.voluntaryarts.org, lists most of the umbrella bodies working in this field in the UK and in other parts of Europe. The list ranges from the Guild of Enamellers to Women in Music and most things in between.

If you want to volunteer in your own neighbourhood, get in touch with your local authority's leisure services officer who might be able to point you in the right direction. Look around to see if there is a local theatre company that needs help putting on a production or getting more young people involved in acting.

Many towns and villages will have an amateur dramatics society or a choral or musical group of some kind that probably needs volunteers. You don't need acting or musical abilities to sell tickets, work front of house or paint scenery, just enthusiasm.

Alternatively, some organisations require musicians to give lessons to those from disadvantaged backgrounds, or those living in hostels or at centres for people with disabilities. There may also be opportunities to support people already working as art and music therapists.

Anyone with a passion for heritage could start their search for voluntary ideas on the website for English Heritage, the government body that protects and promotes the historic environment. The organisation will provide an overview of the sector and offer advice on historic sites that may fire your enthusiasm. It also has a section on community work, which contains advice on setting up your own project, such as creating a heritage trail of places with local or historic importance, or an arts-based project that uses the historic environment in some way.

If you enjoy museums, there might be one locally, or perhaps a cultural centre in your area that needs help. Alternatively, contact the Museum Association or the British Association of Friends of Museums for ideas and tips.

The National Trust is another body that needs volunteers to help to manage its historic sites, from running the gift shop to helping with conservation work.

If you want to combine your passion for literature with fundraising, then volunteering at an Oxfam bookshop could be ideal. These charity shops are appearing across the UK and rely heavily on volunteers to talk to customers, work the till, price stock or organise displays. You don't need to be an expert in the book market, although this could be a good way of using your knowledge to help others.

SUZANNE TROTTER, 29, is an advertising planning executive. She volunteers at the local hospital radio station.

I really love music, so being a DJ for a hospital radio station comes out of a passion for that. I'd wanted to do it for ages and it took some time to find a hospital that needed people, but I've been doing a weekly show at UCL Hospital for three years now.

We'll go around the wards, chat to the patients about their requests and then go back to the studio and put the hour-long show together. We get asked for all kinds of records - lots of middle-of-the-road things and old stuff like Dean Martin and Frank Sinatra. Last year lots of people asked for James Blunt. Involving the patients is a way of keeping their mind off the fact they're in hospital and on something positive. Everyone likes talking about music. It cheers them up.

My work gives me two days off a year to volunteer so earlier this week we went to the hospital and put together a show for the people on the younger wards. There were quizzes and a jingle competition and special guests - the actress who plays the football manager Hazel in 'Footballers' Wives' came along to give out the prizes.

I already do a club night as a DJ and I play music for friends' parties so I already knew what to do, but the first time in the studio is really nerve-racking. Talking and using the equipment at the same time is much harder than you think. I found it really strange to be speaking into a microphone and not seeing who I was chatting to. I wondered if I'd ever get the hang of it but it gets easier over time. You have to learn how to speak slowly and clearly. I've a lot more respect for the DJs I hear on the radio - it is a lot more difficult than you think.

Campaigning

The Make Poverty History campaign in 2005 was an example of what can be achieved when thousands of passionate volunteers get together to lobby governments and try to make a difference to the lives of millions of people around the world.

That campaign, and the subsequent one in 2006 to remind politicians what they agreed to do the year before, needed volunteers to lobby their MPs to cancel Third World debt and raise awareness of poverty issues in their local communities. It also needed people to attend rallies and a protest march to coincide with the G8 summit, which was held in Scotland.

Most political movements and campaigning groups rely heavily on the efforts of volunteers on both a national and a local scale. Getting involved with a group of this kind is a great way to meet people with the same passions as you and with a desire to challenge existing policies and fight injustice. Whatever your area of interest there will probably be a campaigning group that will provide an outlet to make a difference.

Some of the larger organisations, such as Oxfam, the World Development Movement, Greenpeace and Amnesty International are always keen to attract volunteers. Most organisations need administrative help in their national or regional offices for perhaps a day or a morning a week. Tasks could include stuffing envelopes or monitoring the press coverage of their work, for example.

Local representatives are also needed to take the charity's message into their communities, perhaps through organising fundraising activities, putting up posters around town, or setting up an information stall outside a supermarket or library. All these things are key to building the profile of the organisation at grassroots level.

However, campaigning volunteering is not just about raising awareness about international issues. There is plenty to work on in the UK. Homeless charities, for example, need people to raise awareness of the lack of suitable housing, lobby their MPs, or protest about properties that are standing empty while people sleep on the streets. They also need people to highlight the work they do in their communities and to raise money.

In the same way, charities supporting older people, such as Age Concern, need volunteers to help to fight their corner in the political arena and to raise awareness of issues facing the older generation.

CAROLYNN HANSON, 16, is a student from London. She volunteers for Love Music Hate Racism.

We are a small charity, but one that tries to bring people and communities together by organising events. We organise gigs and carnivals, run stalls at fetes, things like that. For the past three years we've organised the large concert in Trafalgar Square on May Day. Love Music Hate Racism is a UK-wide organisation, but the people I know concentrate on London. There's a large concentration in my particular area because the BNP has a lot of councillors here, which concerns us. We've been doing quite a lot of campaigning against them.

We don't organise protests, but when other groups in the community organise them we help to promote them and generate some support. We contact everyone in the group and say, 'This is going to happen – if you're interested, come along and show your support.'

We had two events at schools in the summer of 2006, one in my school. At my school Ms Dynamite came to talk to the children and gave a speech about the importance of embracing other people and how differences should be seen as a beautiful gift and not something to be criticised.

Because it was at my school I was the one who first talked to my headteacher to suggest the idea. He was enthusiastic and after that two employees of Love Music Hate Racism talked to him and worked out the details.

I don't do something every week. There are monthly meetings that I attend for a couple of hours and it depends what events we have on. Every other weekend there might be an event to help out at. Over the holidays I might work in the office for a couple of days. If we have a gig then I will come along before and set up the stall.

I've been involved with Love Music Hate Racism for almost two years. I heard about one of the gigs it was putting on in Trafalgar Square and there was a musical artist I was interested in. My friends and I also wanted to know about the cause and what they did. We phoned them up for more information and they said why not come down and help, so four of us ended up going down, met everyone and ran two stalls. We worked for about eight hours and got to see all the artists. It was really good fun, and we kept in contact with the organisation.

I have a lot of fun with the people I work with, but it can be difficult. You do get some abuse from people when you're out leafleting, some can be quite hard to deal with. But when there's a gig or carnival, there is such a nice atmosphere.

I'm white, but I have got Asian and Muslim friends, and my school is quite diverse. Some of the abuse my friends have received I'm really uncomfortable with. There is definitely a reason why it is this particular cause I am involved in.

Children and young people

Organisations that work with children, young people and families often need volunteers to run clubs, supervise activities, or help with mentoring schemes.

Schools are often keen to take volunteers, particularly to offer support to children with special educational needs or pupils who need help with reading. The organisation Reading Volunteers brings volunteers together with children in primary schools to help them develop new reading skills and increase their confidence. Volunteers need only give one hour a week, and because they receive training no experience is required. Similar programmes offer focused support for children in care.

Alternatively, specific charities need volunteers to take their message into schools, perhaps through assemblies or in class, or to encourage headteachers to get involved in new initiatives. Save the Children, for example, needs school link promoters to interest local primary schools in participating in a project that teaches children about the daily lives of other young people living in developing countries, and in how the charity helps to improve their lives.

Other schemes involving young people could involve working with crime prevention organisations, which need mentors to spend time with young people at risk of turning to crime.

With some training, you could get involved with a mentoring scheme that supports young people recovering from mental health problems, helping them to achieve their full potential in education and work. This kind of support can be vital in helping youngsters to regain confidence.

31-year-old JAMES FERGUSON, from Yorkshire, works part time and is studying to become a youth counsellor. He volunteers with young people, especially those at risk of offending.

About four or five years ago I was working full time in a call centre and I decided I wanted a change in career and to work with young people. So I found the number for the local youth offending service from Yellow Pages and contacted them to see if there were any opportunities for volunteering. I knew that without any qualifications, volunteering was the only way to get experience, because I couldn't go back to college. They asked if I could volunteer for 12 months, but in the end I did two years. It was really, really good. I met a lot of great young people and got a lot of positive results out of the work.

I met kids who were either first-time offenders or at risk of offending. They had been referred by parents, schools or the police. I was working with them on a one-to-one basis to see things from their point of view and let them talk to me. In a way my job was to be someone they could sound off to.

I was able to put a lot of my own personality into it. I worked about three hours a week on average, which is not a great deal of time but it can really help a young person.

After two years I moved on to a youth engagement scheme - a New Deal for Communities programme. As well as still doing part-time work at the call centre, I was working at a comprehensive school as part of the engagement programme and I also went back to college to do a counselling course. I'm aiming to become a counsellor specialising in working with young people. I now volunteer for about eight hours a week for which I get paid out-of-pocket expenses.

It is something I have always been interested in and wanted to do. I could easily spend about five hours playing computer games at the weekend, which is daft. I thought, surely I could use those five hours more constructively and positively with young people?

Volunteering for me just ticks all the boxes, apart from earning money - there's job satisfaction, feedback, challenges, trying to raise other people's expectations of themselves. And it also gives you extra things to put on your CV and you make contacts. It is whatever you choose to make it.

A lot of women volunteer, and they do a fantastic job, but 99 per cent of the young people are lads. Most are from one-parent families, where their dad's not there and they really want a man who will listen to them.

Emergency and rescue services

Despite the highly specialised nature of the emergency services, they are still reliant on the support of volunteers. Getting involved in this area can be immensely rewarding and offers good work experience if you want a career in the emergency services. Even with training and support, volunteering in this field does involve an element of danger and may need a little extra thought before you sign up.

The Fire Brigade has 18,200 retained officers in the UK, many of whom live in more rural areas where there aren't full-time crews. Although not volunteers in the traditional sense of the word, retained officers are men and women who are trained in using the same equipment as the full-time force and are 'on call' day and night to attend emergencies. Most work full time but have an arrangement with their employer that when their bleeper goes off they have to leave work. So, if you want to get involved you need to have a sympathetic employer and be someone who can cope with the unpredictable nature of the work.

As well as attending call-outs, which could average two to three times a week, you will be required to attend weekly training sessions. You will be paid a regular 'retaining fee' and will receive money every time you are called out.

The retained force may also be required to promote fire safety at local events and in schools. Airfield volunteer fire rescue groups also exist around the country, assisting at aviation events.

The police force has a similar band of volunteers, known as special constables, who back up the work of full-time officers. After some initial training in basic police work, such as learning about common crimes and the powers of arrest and self-defence, the 'specials' agree to volunteer for a minimum of four hours a week at their local police station. The Metropolitan Police may ask for more.

Special constables have the same powers as a regular officer, and wear a similar uniform. Their role is to provide a link between the local police force and the community. This will often mean patrolling the streets, assisting at crime scenes and tackling anti-social behaviour, so you'll need patience, tact and good communication skills, as well as good physical health. The work you do, however, will depend on the force in which you are based.

The key difference between the retained fire brigade and police specials is that police specials are not usually paid. Some forces are introducing some form of wage, but you would need to check with your local force. Again, volunteers will be required to update their skills with regular training sessions, and there could be opportunities for promotion within the special force.

For the more medically minded, voluntary opportunities can be found with the St John Ambulance, which provides first aid and medical services at public events across the country. Volunteers can also teach first aid courses, help with medical programmes for the homeless and offer support to young carers. The organisation recruits volunteers from as young as five and you don't have to commit a specific time each week to help out. First aid training will be given.

If you live near the sea, voluntary opportunities exist within the Royal National Lifeboat Institution (RNLI), which provides 24-hour lifesaving services around the UK and Ireland. The RNLI needs volunteers for its lifeboat crews and to help run the lifeboat station and assist with launches. It also needs lifeguards and local fundraisers. With training, anyone between the ages of 17 and 55 can become a crew member, providing they are physically fit. Alternatively, if you live near mountains, consider joining their local Mountain Rescue group. Volunteers need to be at least 18, be fit and healthy, be competent navigators, have some technical skills, such as in rope work, and possess a first aid qualification. Initial and ongoing training will be given.

NETTY (54) and CHRIS (58) HEDGES, from Orpington, Kent, have volunteered with the Red Cross for more than 30 years. They were on duty at Waterloo Place for the VJ celebrations when they were deployed on a Red Cross ambulance to the bus bomb in London on July 7 2005.

We got the call about 9.30 a.m. and were deployed to Tavistock Square where the bus was.

It must have been around 10 a.m. when we arrived. A lot of the seriously injured had already been taken to hospital. There were a lot of people with minor injuries who were very distressed.

It seemed to be a very controlled scene. Everybody was calmer than you would imagine. The police, London Ambulance Service and other volunteers were all doing their jobs very efficiently. We were able to put our training in place.

We helped a young woman who had minor injuries and then went into shock. She actually passed out when she was taken into Tavistock House, an office nearby. She was still unconscious when we arrived to treat her.

We were then deployed to another casualty who had not been directly involved in the bombing but she was very distressed by all the people walking everywhere. We saw a lot of traumatised people and dealt with another person who had collapsed from shock in the street.

We have never been involved in an incident like that before - not to that extent.

But it has been something we have all been training for and everything ran very smoothly. Everybody who had been trained to deal with a major incident put the plans into operation quite quickly and it worked. I just hope we never have to deal with this again - once was enough.

Environment and conservation

With an ever-growing interest in environmental issues among politicians and the public, there are lots of opportunities for you to get involved in green projects, whether that means doing conservation work in your local area or on a wider scale for national heritage organisations. You can help with administration tasks, get stuck into building, clearing or cleaning projects, or monitor changes to environmental sites and gather data. Many conservation organisations have projects for volunteers, lasting from one day to several weeks. Some also offer working holidays, either in the UK or overseas. Vocational training courses, particularly tailored for unemployed people, are also available at some charities.

Consider getting involved with Encams, formerly known as The Tidy Britain Group, or get involved in the Britain in Bloom competition or litter-picking campaigns in your neighbourhood.

National organisations, such as Friends of the Earth or Greenpeace, are crying out for help to promote their aims and keep environmental issues on the government agenda. Voluntary work could involve lobbying MPs, taking part in demonstrations or fundraising.

If you are interested in sustainable transport, why not become a volunteer ranger for Sustrans, which is coordinating the National Cycle Network. Rangers help to monitor and maintain sections of the network that are close to their homes.

Volunteers can also combine their ecological interests with a trip overseas as many charities now offer conservation holidays abroad. The expedition organisation Frontier, for example, works with local governments, NGOs and communities overseas to help to tackle conservation problems. It offers longer-term opportunities in countries such as Fiji, Tanzania, Cambodia and Nicaragua.

JANET ALTY, 69, is a retired further education teacher. She volunteers for many environmental and community causes.

I can honestly say that volunteering has been one of the guiding forces in my life. For me it is about taking social justice and responsibility, both locally and globally. It is phenomenal what individuals can do. I feel like I'm engaged in society. I don't do it to be known. I just like the idea that I'm having an effect. I have three grandchildren and I want them to think that when I go to my grave I did my best, for them and for the planet.

People used to mock the green movement. They used to laugh about people knitting lentils and growing organic food but now it is become more mainstream. I've been a member of the Green Party since 1987. For me it is about having Labour values in global terms. After all it is no good having the values if you no longer have a planet to put them into action on. It is about equity – a fair chance for all on a global scale.

I'm a member of a group called Action 21. It does all kinds of things, from helping people with little money to grow food on allotments to carrying out research into wind turbines and persuading the local Grade 2 listed church to have ground source heating. It is about waking people up to ideas. I'm also involved in Living Streets, which campaigns for better rights for pedestrians, plus a group which has built links between Leamington Spa and a town called Bo in Sierra Leone for the last 25 years. Some of the people I've met feel like family. I've been there twice and I'd return tomorrow if I could.

One of the biggest projects I've taken on is being chairman of the local Single Regeneration board, a scheme that was originally set up under John Major. We've

attempted to improve one of the poorest areas in the whole of Warwickshire, socially, environmentally and economically.

I've always had a sense that I'm part of society and had friends from all walks of life. Perhaps it is because I come from a Scottish background where people are not so obsessed by class like they are in England. One of the earliest volunteering projects I did was in the seventies with some local Punjabi women. They were isolated at home and unable to speak English. We encouraged people to go into their homes and teach them, make friends with them. I swear it was a seminal moment in our community. It changed people's attitudes and some of those women are still my friends now.

Health and social care

There are numerous health and social care charities working to better the lives of people from all sections of the community who are coping with illness, disabilities or emotional difficulties and the volunteering opportunities in this field are wide and varied. While some training may be required, a sense of compassion and patience are vital if you want to get involved.

Hospitals and hospices often require the services of volunteers to help brighten up the lives of their patients or those receiving palliative care. Opportunities can include visiting patients who perhaps don't have many callers, presenting a show on hospital radio or working in reception at your local hospice.

Hospices care for people with advanced terminal illness, supporting them and their families. Volunteers are considered a vital part of the team, supporting the work of paid staff through administration and housekeeping tasks, or driving families to and from the hospice for days out. People with a background in social work or counselling could also find their services in demand at their local hospice.

Some organisations work to educate people on health matters, as well as offering support to those in need. Children with Aids, for example, helps children and families touched by HIV and Aids by providing hardship support and education programmes.

If you want to offer more emotional support, consider working with the Samaritans, which provides confidential support all day, every day, or Childline, which is a free, confidential helpline for children and young people in distress.

There are also similar services for people who are experiencing homophobia or domestic violence. There are other organisations that counsel victims of rape and other crimes.

People suffering from mental illness also need your support. If you are a man living in London, why not consider volunteering for TimeBank's Back to Life mentoring scheme, which supports young men recovering from mental health problems. Male volunteers are paired up with men of a similar age to support them get back into education or employment.

The mental health charity Mind, which promotes inclusion and seeks to influence policy through lobbying and education programmes, requires volunteers to campaign on their behalf and organise fundraising events.

Perhaps you could consider befriending someone who is lonely, offering them companionship and taking them on outings and to social events.

Less hands-on practical work can be found in the regional and national offices of charities, which often need volunteers to carry out administrative tasks. For example, Macmillan Cancer Relief, which supports people with cancer and their families, often needs people to undertake administrative work and staff telephone helplines.

Other organisations require volunteers to support families with young children who are affected by mental or physical illness, poverty or isolation, or who just find it difficult coping with parenthood. Home-Start has some 11,000 volunteers around the UK who offer emotional and physical support to parents through home and family visits and organised day trips. You don't usually need any specific qualifications to become a volunteer in this area, just experience of being a full-time carer of children. You may only need to volunteer for a couple of hours a week.

Volunteering could be ideal if you are considering a career in the field of health or social care. Not only will it give you experience of the sector, but the training you may be required to undertake could lead to a recognised qualification, perhaps in counselling.

Homelessness and housing

Organisations that work in this area often require volunteers to help with fundraising, offer administrative support or work in drop-in centres or on outreach projects. Charities that support the homeless tend to be based in cities, so this may be a consideration if you decide you want to get involved.

As well as the larger charities, such as Shelter, Crisis, St Mungo's and Centrepoint, there are many smaller groups helping homeless people in their own communities by cooking meals in local hostels, providing medical care or helping people to fill in application forms for work and benefits.

For example, the social care organisation the Oasis Trust, based in London, offers accommodation to young women who have found themselves homeless. The trust provides a structured programme for up to 14 women between the ages of 16 and 25, to help them get an education, a job and a home of their own.

Getting involved with these smaller organisations may allow you to do more hands-on work and give you a real sense that you are doing something valuable for marginalised members of society. Your local authority or volunteer centre should be able to provide details of any community projects that support the homeless.

That's not to say that the larger national organisations should be ignored. Not only do they need volunteers to raise funds – some offer places in the London Marathon or other major sporting events on the condition that you raise a set amount of money for them – they also need people to work in their charity shops or volunteer at their hostels.

Every Christmas, Crisis needs more than 5,000 volunteers to help to run the London centres that it sets up to provide shelter, support and companionship to the homeless or those living in hostels over the festive season.

St Mungo's often needs enthusiastic volunteers to run activity sessions for a few hours a week at its hostels and drop-in centres. It also needs those with good interpersonal skills to offer support to homeless people.

Shelter requires volunteers who can work as researchers or advisers or in one of its charity shops, which could lead to a National Vocational Qualification (NVQ).

These charities are also involved in making the issues of homelessness and poor housing – and its effects on the individual – more high profile through campaigning and lobbying the government.

SHARON MCCORMACK, 44, works for a scheme providing support for the long-term unemployed. She volunteers for Shelter Families Project in Blantyre, South Lanarkshire.

Sometimes it is difficult to find volunteer work that you can fit around being a mother, but the Shelter Families Project has been brilliant – I've been able to finish my social sciences degree, look after my 12-year-old son AND work for the charity. In many ways, it has changed my life as much as the lives of the families who need help. I used to wear a suit and work in a bank. Now I've got a new job working with the long-term unemployed. Without the experience I got volunteering I doubt I'd have been as confident in the interview – I just understood all the issues so much better. The whole experience of volunteering has done my confidence the world of good.

The scheme works by providing both practical and emotional support to homeless families. It might be helping them out moving into new accommodation – painting and decorating, sorting out tenancy agreements, finding a nursery in the new area. Or it might be offering emotional support and friendship – often people are moving to a new area where they might feel vulnerable or lonely. Often they will have been in Bed and Breakfast accommodation or temporary lodgings for months on end. Other support networks might have washed their hands of them and we're the only ones they can turn to.

Some of the people we see are single mothers who have escaped from violent relationships. Being a mum myself really helps me to understand the pressures they're under. They're so used to being judged, their self-esteem and confidence is at rock bottom. it has been a long time since they've had anyone on their side. One mum told me that without our non-judgemental support she thought she'd have committed suicide.

It is all very well reading about people with housing crises in a book like I did when I was doing my degree. The reality is very different. But at least I feel that I've been able to offer some support in some way. I've got a lot more out of it than I ever bargained for.

Mentoring

A mentor acts as a role model to help another person to discover and achieve their goals, through encouragement, guidance and a listening ear. This sort of work is often performed on a one-to-one basis, which can be quite tough, but at the same time immensely rewarding.

Mentors are usually needed to encourage people who are going through a particularly difficult time in their life, such as recovering from an illness, or who are at risk of social exclusion, falling into crime or some form of substance abuse. Mentors are also needed to support young people preparing to leave care, or to improve levels of achievement among school pupils with learning difficulties, who might find it hard to mix with other children. Mentees can be all ages and from all backgrounds.

Mentors are also needed in the workplace. Experienced professionals are often asked to mentor a new recruit or trainee, providing a first port of call if problems arise as they settle in. This type of work usually requires a monthly or bi-monthly commitment to meet and discuss any concerns.

The crucial skills needed by would-be mentors are the ability to communicate well and to listen carefully. If you have been in a difficult situation yourself, perhaps having been caught up in crime as a youngster, and feel motivated to prevent others from doing the same, you could make an ideal mentor. Who better to warn others of the pitfalls and understand the issues they are facing than someone who has already been there?

LAURENCE DIPROSE, 33, from Bournemouth, volunteers for Nacro's Football Foundation project.

I do football coaching, take team sessions and mentor youngsters who are risk of offending, or kids who are affected by substance misuse in Bournemouth. I also do a bit of refereeing if there's a tournament.

I got involved with Nacro after I'd gone into recovery. I was involved in substance abuse in a heavy way for 15 years. It was quite bad and led me to some not very nice places. I thought I would like to give a bit back and help kids who were going through things I had been going through. I've been involved with the football foundation for about two years. They've trained me up, so I'm now qualified as a level one coach, so I can take my own football sessions. I also volunteer as a mentor – that's what I would like to do as a career. I work as a part-time youth worker, a job I got through my involvement with Nacro, and I'm training to be a youth worker full time.

I wish there had been something like this around for me when I was younger. If I had known about stuff like this it would have helped with my self-esteem. When you're in that state your self-esteem is on the floor. If I'd read in a book that someone was going through what I went through and could come through the other side, that would definitely have helped me.

The young people seem to trust you more because they know where you come from. I can tell them I was brought up in the same environment. I have had cards from kids thanking me. The work is relationship-building really. And the kids can take a lot of their anger on to the football pitch, rather than smashing something or someone up. Being involved with Nacro has definitely helped my career, and my confidence is absolutely booming. I've just won a Nacro volunteering award.

Older people

Organisations that provide help to older people usually need volunteers to work at lunch clubs, help in care homes, or transport those who are unable to drive to and from a function or to the hospital or doctor's surgery for medical care. Some simply need volunteers to spend time with an older person who perhaps has no close friends or family, or who is unable to leave their home very often due to illness.

More than that, though, volunteers are needed to make older people feel valued in a society that seems to be more interested in youth. Why not get in touch with your local residential care home to ask if it needs any help. If you are musical, perhaps you could entertain residents. If you're a hairdresser, consider using your skills to offer free haircuts. Alternatively, if you know an older person who lives nearby, see if they would like company. If they do, make regular visits. Perhaps you could host coffee mornings or afternoon teas.

Some older people with pets might need help looking after them. The Cinnamon Trust organises volunteers to take dogs for walks or look after pets if the owner has to go into hospital.

If you want something less hands-on, you could offer your services to a local charity shop that supports older people, such as Help the Aged, or work in an organisation's head office. You could also get involved in campaigning. Some charities, such as Action on Elder Abuse, which works to protect and prevent the abuse of older people, is campaigning for legislation to protect the elderly from harm in their own homes, in residential care homes or in hospital. Why not help to promote the cause?

NATALIE SAVONA, 39, is a nutritionist and writer. She volunteers for Age Concern.

I first met Dorothy four years ago as a result of calling my local branch of Age Concern and asking them if there was anyone in the area who would appreciate a visit. She's 95 years old. While she's not typical in many ways – she can afford to heat her bungalow and can survive on her pension – she does need company

because none of her relatives live nearby. You realise that all the money in the world doesn't stop you being lonely.

She isn't the type to sit and watch television all day. We'll have a natter over a cup of tea and a saffron bun. What she likes best is a long drive out into the countryside. She'll tell me where the best bluebell woods are or point out abandoned old train lines. If we're not in the car on our three-hour drives I'll take her to the supermarket or we'll go to the library and she'll change her library books. I try to prompt her a bit. If her teeth are playing up I'll say 'Come on, we need to go to the dentist.'

She's got a fantastic memory and she was plainly quite an adventurer in her day. She used to be a school teacher and is not fazed by anything. Sometimes she's a bit crotchety or in a bad mood. But then we all are sometimes. I challenge her quite a lot. I can be cheeky with her or tease her and she doesn't seem to mind. It is an equal sort of relationship.

I guess I'm motivated by a complete terror of growing old and being frail and lonely. I've always hated to see elderly people disregarded or ignored. If I'm feeling vulnerable and I see an elderly person struggling on their own I will burst into tears. It is something that strikes a chord with me.

We tend to disown the elderly in this country, or write them off as utterly useless. Yet if you read any spiritual books it is always the older people who are the most prized members of society, treasured for their wisdom. I think we've lost a lot of that attitude. We all want things now, this instant. The idea of valuing experience has diminished. But we forget about the old at our peril.

I love hearing Dorothy's stories about growing up. Part of me is quite old-fashioned myself – I think it would be tragic if these elderly lives were cast aside. This is my tiny way of not doing that, of respecting elderly people. When I go to see her I feel virtuous and I also enjoy myself. I feel as if I've contributed to somebody's day. When I'm too busy to see her, the guilt sets in, but to tell you the truth it is my loss if I don't go.

Sometimes I think if the age groups mixed more – elderly people spent time with children and vice versa – then the world would be a much better place. There's so much potential there. It doesn't have to be a one-way street.

People with disabilities

There are numerous ways to provide support in this area, from fundraising to offering respite care. For example, you could support adults with disabilities who are taking classes at a local college. This could involve transporting them to classes or assisting them while in lessons. Children and young people with disabilities may also require support if they want to go to after-school clubs or youth clubs.

If you can dedicate a block of time, perhaps two weeks, to volunteering, many charities need help with taking people with disabilities on holiday. These trips offer the person a break and their full-time carers some respite. Visualise, formerly the Winged Fellowship Trust, is one of the organisations looking for volunteers to help in this way.

Organisations like the Community Service Volunteers need volunteers to offer support to families with members who have physical disabilities. This kind of work requires good communication skills and sometimes specific skills, such as sign language.

Other charities work to encourage independence among those who have physical disabilities. The Back-Up Trust, for example, supports people with spinal cord injuries, and seeks to improve their self-confidence and motivation after the traumatic life-changing incident that led to the injury. It offers mentoring programmes and training in how to use wheelchairs across different terrains. It also organises outward-bound activity days, weekends and longer residential events, and arranges skiing holidays. All of these projects need volunteers.

If you know British Sign Language, think about using your skills to interpret for someone who is deaf or hard of hearing, perhaps while they are at school or attending an event. Or perhaps you could consider volunteering for the RNIB's Talking Book Service, a postal lending library of audio books that are delivered through the post to more than 40,000 blind and partially sighted people throughout the UK. Volunteers are needed to install new audio players or demonstrate how the library works to new customers. If you want a bit more responsibility, you could become a volunteer coordinator to provide a link between the RNIB headquarters and a local team of volunteers, and help to train and support volunteers in their work.

RAY EDWARDS is a quad amputee who volunteers for the Limbless Association.

In 1987 I became a quad amputee through septicaemia. I was in the hospital unit and there was a leaflet for the Limbless Association. I just happened to look at it, talked to someone and thought it was a good idea to become a member.

I am a member and a volunteer, and I was a trustee, but I felt the need to do more so I decided to resign my position as a trustee and become the deputy CEO as well as the Disabled Centres Coordinator.

A volunteer offers support. I never thought there were people who could give advice to someone in my situation: there weren't too many people when I first became disabled who had lost both arms and legs. It was daunting.

A volunteer might get a phone call from the association in their local area in response to a call from someone who is about to become an amputee, or from an amputee who is finding life a bit difficult. The volunteer will visit or call, and reassure them that it is not that bad. To some people losing a limb can be like a bereavement. We have an army of people across the UK who can offer support to amputees, wherever they are.

It is down to the individual of course – sometimes you can lead a horse to water but you can't make it drink. You can tell a person that it can be OK to be an amputee, but it is down to that person whether or not they take that on board. I must say that when I lost all four limbs I was devastated and I just wanted to give up. When you have lost something yourself, you really are able to give your thoughts to someone who is suffering from the same trauma.

I came from a building background and as well as my work for the Limbless Association I am the managing director of a building company that adapts houses for the disabled. I wanted to give something back to society and I think that through the Association and my specialist company I'm able to do that.

The Limbless Association provides comprehensive back-up to help enhance the lives of amputees. Everything that a human being needs after an amputation we should be able to give them, or put them on the right path. The helpline is always fairly busy and we publish a quarterly magazine as well.

It is hard to judge how many of our volunteers are amputees – we have 3,700 members so a high percentage of those volunteering their time are amputees themselves.

I'd love to increase the size of the organisation, get a greater profile and make people aware that we are there for them. As a quad amputee I think I am a good ambassador for the Association.

Prisoners, ex-offenders and crime prevention

Offering support to prisoners and their families can be challenging and requires a great deal of sensitivity. However, it can be tremendously rewarding. There are a number of ways you can get involved in this field, from writing letters or visiting prisoners to advocating penal reform.

The first step is to contact your local prison to see what particular help it needs. It may, for example, have a visitors' centre which needs volunteers to serve tea and coffee, create a welcoming atmosphere, and perhaps offer a listening ear for the often forgotten families who have to cope with a relative's imprisonment. With some training, you may be able to advise visitors on how they can get financial help for their visits or what they can and can't take into the prison. Some prisons may have facilities for children, which will need volunteers. The Prison Advice and Care Trust offers good advice on how to get started on volunteering in this area.

The National Association of Official Prison Visitors coordinates the activities of visitors, who agree to meet a prisoner on a regular basis, regardless of whether they have family or friends. Volunteers will need to be patient, respectful and be good listeners. You will receive training and support from the association.

Prisoners Abroad needs volunteers to write to, or translate documents for, Britons who are jailed overseas. The organisation works with those already convicted or awaiting trial and makes no moral judgements over whether someone is innocent or guilty, so you will need to look elsewhere if you want to campaign on behalf of an individual. There are opportunities to visit a prisoner overseas, although this must be handled with sensitivity and it would be worth speaking to the British consulate before arranging a visit. Less direct action could involve working in the organisation's London head office.

The relatives of prisoners can often be forgotten, but as well as practical support during visiting hours, some need support when they get back home. The Prisoners' Families Helpline offers free, confidential support to those finding it hard to cope after a relative has been sent to prison. Volunteers work out of two centres, in Manchester and Cambridge, and should be able to give two to four hours a week, ideally for six months. You will need to undergo training before you start work.

Once someone leaves prison, they will need help and support to readjust back into society. The crime reduction charity Nacro recruits volunteers for a number of tasks, such as mentoring adults while they are in prison and after they are released. The organisation is also involved in crime prevention, so you could volunteer to coach a football team for young people who are at risk of getting involved with crime.

If you have a cool head, perhaps you could get involved in mediation, that is intervening in disputes between neighbours. Other options include getting involved with your local neighbourhood watch group, perhaps by organising or providing a venue for meetings, liaising with police officers or simply delivering leaflets about the organisation to your neighbours.

Refugees and asylum seekers

Volunteering opportunities with refugees and those seeking asylum usually involve offering practical as well as emotional support.

Negative publicity surrounding the issue of asylum has given rise to some false perceptions of refugees. Volunteering for a refugee charity or NGO can give you a better understanding of the issues and difficulties the majority of those seeking asylum will face.

Volunteering opportunities could include working in a support centre for refugees, perhaps collating information for new arrivals, offering them cultural advice and orientation services as they adjust to life in a new country. You could find yourself filling in official documents or teaching English.

Volunteers are needed from the moment an asylum seeker steps off the plane. The Refugee Arrivals Project has offices at Heathrow airport to offer immediate support and practical help to those claiming asylum, helping them to find emergency accommodation or putting them in contact with friends or family who might be in the UK. The organisation has a volunteering arm called Amigos, which provides one-to-one support to asylum seekers.

The Refugee Council has offices across England which need volunteers in order to function effectively. It divides its volunteers into three areas - volunteering in direct services, office-based volunteering and community-based volunteering. If you become a direct service volunteer you could give English lessons, help project workers to advise asylum seekers, or serve meals in a day centre. If you're an office-based volunteer you might be involved in researching projects, writing articles for newsletters, helping out at events or undertaking general administrative tasks. As the name suggests, community volunteering is helping to organise events or projects that support asylum seekers where they are living. So, this could mean you will be involved in running a women's group, coaching a football team, or accompanying people to appointments or meetings. It could also involve dispelling the myths about asylum seekers by giving talks and presentations in your community.

If you want to make a long-term commitment to assist just one refugee, then consider volunteering for TimeBank's Time Together scheme, which matches a refugee with a UK citizen who then provides mentoring support for about five hours a month for a year. As a mentor, you could help your mentee to write a CV, visit local museums or areas of interest, and advise them on cultural customs and practices.

If you are a social work student or thinking of working with refugees full time, volunteering is a great way to get practical experience, while helping people at perhaps one of the loneliest and most traumatic times of their lives.

LOUISE FRANCE, 39, is a journalist. She volunteers for TimeBank's Time Together, a charity which teams refugees up with mentors.

I'd become more and more alarmed about the xenophobic way refugees are written about in the press. Historically we're a country made up of all kinds of nationalities and that's something I've always been very proud of. I also kept thinking - imagine what it would be like turning up somewhere where you know no one, where you're traumatised by the country you've left and the country you've arrived in is, at best, unfriendly and unhelpful. I get nervous and tongue-tied in Paris, let alone somewhere even more alien.

Time Together is a scheme which helps refugees to survive in Britain. Each volunteer is allotted a mentee over 12 months. The idea is to help them with whatever they need - job applications, English lessons, orientation around London. It might just be explaining a particularly idiosyncratic British custom.

My mentee is a wonderful woman called Marjan. We're the same age, the same sex, but our lives have been very different. She was a doctor in Afghanistan. She has four children, the eldest is 17. She fled Afghanistan over 12 years ago when her father was killed. It has been very hard for her since she arrived here but she's managed to keep her family together and she just doggedly seems to refuse to give up.

I've helped her fill in forms and apply for college courses. She practises her

English, which is already remarkably good (I'm always telling her my Urdu is non-existent). She's incredibly warm and appreciative. Somehow, despite our contrasting life experiences, we've quickly formed a bond. We laugh a lot, which is a good sign.

I've never done any volunteer work before but I wish I'd started years ago. I work from home and often spend hours on my own. When I meet Marjan she lights up the day. She's always sending me texts saying how grateful she is for my help. I wonder if she realises how much she's added to my life too.

Sport

Up to 1.5 million volunteers are already involved in running community sports events in England alone. You don't need to be David Beckham or Paula Radcliffe to get involved in sports volunteering. All you need is bags of enthusiasm and a passion to see people reach their full sporting potential.

If sports volunteering is something you want to explore, think about what you can contribute. Are you good at a particular sport, or do you have a coaching qualification? If so, contact your local sports club to see if they need help. If you don't have any coaching certificates, contact the national body of your chosen sport to see what is on offer. Age is no bar, as many governing bodies offer leadership qualifications to young people which could be the first step on the ladder to coaching or officiating.

Many areas of the country will have established clubs in the major sports, such as football, rugby, netball and swimming, but if your interests lie elsewhere, perhaps in fencing or trampolining, and there isn't a club already set up, why not establish one yourself? There are more details about doing it yourself on page 71. The same advice applies for setting up a sports club as any other volunteering association, except that you will, of course, need at least one trained coach in your club to be covered by insurance and to teach those who attend properly.

If your interest in sport is more behind the scenes, clubs need treasurers, administrators, caretakers and someone to provide the all-important half-time snack or end-of-season medals, so there are plenty of opportunities. If you have a car, you could provide transport for away matches or competitions.

If you have a financial background, you could help a local club to raise money. There are plenty of government and lottery grants now available for local clubs. The problem is that many of the people involved in running them don't have the time to fill in long, sometimes complicated, application forms. If you have experience of applying for funding in this way, perhaps in the course of your work, you will be welcomed with open arms by a small club in need of some money to help build an indoor pitch, or running track, or pay for new equipment.

As we count down to the London Olympic and Paralympic games in 2012, thousands of volunteers will be needed to carry out a range of tasks. The events may still be years away, but the Olympic committee is already predicting that the games will need up to 70,000 volunteers. Although recruiting will not begin until 2010, you can register your interest on the London 2012 website www.london2012.com now.

KEN LEECH, 59, is a retired hotelier. He is chairman of Kendal Ski Club.

We have all kinds of people coming along wanting to learn to ski. Many of them might have been put off skiing, thinking it is too elitist for them or too expensive. But our volunteers work with everyone - school kids, Brownies, Cub Scouts.

One of the best parts of the work we do is the sessions with people with disabilities. It is an incredibly rare opportunity for disabled people to feel some of the liberation that comes from skiing. They might only slide a couple of metres, but the squeals of delight are amazing. We've even developed a remote control system which means they can control the machinery that tows them up to the top. There's also a group of blind skiers. They bring their buddies who tell them whether to go left a bit or right a bit. It is an incredible thing to watch. But that's the thing about skiing - it is a great leveller. It doesn't matter how clever you are or how wealthy or how fit - everyone falls over sometimes.

The Kendal ski club was begun in 1984. The founders virtually built it with their bare hands and it is had that kind of egalitarian ethos ever since. Nobody at the club gets paid - that's set in stone. There are about 40 instructors, plus another 100 volunteers who help in the club house with maintenance and equipment.

I'd never skied until I was 49 when I came along to Kendal. People think it is a uniquely young people's sport but it is not. There's one man who comes along who is 83. The guys who set it up are now in their 70s and they're still really active here. I never imagined I'd be good enough to teach people but I get a great deal of satisfaction out of it. I'm always on the lookout to convert someone to get more volunteers on board. I get quite evangelical about it. There's a huge mix of us, everyone from builders to doctors. I've made some great friends and in a way it has become a social thing as well as a way to put something back into the local community.

I can still remember the first time I skied down from the top. I remember standing there thinking, 'How on earth am I going to do it?' It isn't far - only 100 metres - but it is pretty steep and can look daunting. But you see people get such an amazing feeling of accomplishment. It is a fantastic confidence booster. To be able to ski - to be at the top of a mountain and have that lovely graceful feeling of skiing down - is something magical.

Trusteeships

A charity's trustees are the people who are legally and financially responsible for its overall management and decision-making. They are, in effect, responsible for the general direction and performance of the charity, so, while ultimately rewarding, the role can be quite challenging.

Becoming a trustee is quite a responsibility, so consider it carefully and choose your charity wisely. You will need to be able to handle the stress that comes with this sort of responsibility – if things go wrong it will be down to you to explain why and help to sort out the problem. The Charity Commission is recommending that all charitable organisations become companies limited by guarantee, which will mean trustees won't be held accountable if something does go wrong financially. This could be a consideration when deciding where you want to work.

If you become a trustee of a smaller charity, you could find yourself more directly involved in day-to-day activities as well as having an overall monitoring role, so make sure you know what will be required of you. Anyone over the age of 18 who has not been convicted of a crime, or involved in deception or dishonesty, or who has declared bankruptcy, can become a trustee. But because of the level of responsibility, a trusteeship is ideal for an older person with a number of years' experience in management or business.

Before taking the plunge, find out as much as you can about the charity. Try to meet the other trustees. Investigate the financial health of the organisation and find out more about its activities. You should also familiarise yourself with the legal and financial liabilities that come with the role. Think also about the time commitment it will involve. Although you might only need to attend two meetings a month, trustees are usually expected to stay in the role for several years. Can you give this type of long-term support?

MADI SHARMA, 43, is an entrepreneur from Nottingham. She does a variety of volunteering work, sitting on boards, promoting entrepreneurship in schools, and speaking out against domestic violence.

I do a whole lot of things. I'm an entrepreneur, an importer of goods from India, but I used to be a food manufacturer with a company I started in my kitchen at home. I went from making four samosas a day to running two factories with 35 staff. That's where the volunteering started. Even for a small company, I knew it was important to get involved in the place where you recruit employees.

I believe that everybody who succeeds should go back to their school and become a governor to say thank you. I went back to my kids' school, which was the same one I attended. Volunteering as a school governor is a good place to start. I then sat on the board of the senior school that I went to.

I was then elected to the parish council, and I was asked to be on taskforces. I'm Asian and female, I'm a single parent and in business, and therefore I tick all the boxes. A lot of people were asking me to help either through charity or to sit on boards. You shouldn't sit on a board unless you have something to say or have an interest in what they are doing. Some people just wanted me because I ticked those boxes.

My advice is to get involved with things that you are passionate about. I love business, but at 16 I was told business was no place for a woman. I now go into schools and talk about how I did it and inspire others.

I'm also on the Duke of Edinburgh women in business panel. I believe youngsters are our future and have so much to offer. It is a great way of teaching citizenship and getting youngsters involved in volunteering at an early age.

People say if you want something doing, ask a busy person. But anyone can give up time out of one day. I don't care what job you are doing, there's no way anyone can't make time to do these sorts of things.

My hero is Mahatma Gandhi, who said you have to be the change you want to see in the world. I get satisfaction that I have made a difference. Every evening I ask myself, what have I achieved today? We're on earth for a reason. If I make a difference to one person's life, I have done what I had to do.

5. Getting started

So, you've decided what you want to put in and get out of volunteering and narrowed down your areas of interest. It is now time to get down to business, make contact and get involved. This book contains a directory of voluntary organisations that take volunteers. But how do you decide which children's charity or environmental organisation to sign up with?

There are a number of ways to make the decision, but one of the best is to get in touch with a charity you're interested in and find out a bit more about their work and how you will be expected to contribute. Many charities and NGOs will have current or past volunteers that you can speak to about the type of work they did and whether they enjoyed it. By doing this, you can get a sense of how the organisation operates.

Alternatively, contact your local volunteer centre, which will offer more impartial advice. TimeBank or www.volunteering.org.uk are also good places to start.

Your local National Association for Voluntary and Community Action (NAVCA) may be able to offer some guidance, particularly if you want to set up your own volunteering group. These councils are made up of local voluntary and community organisations and their main functions are to share good practice, identify opportunities and resources and promote the voluntary sector. It is also worth contacting the head office of a national charity, which could give you a better idea of the work it does in your area.

Umbrella organisations may also be able to help (see page 205 for a list), although their work is more to coordinate the activities and represent the interests of related bodies. For example, the organisation Attend is an umbrella body for health and social care, supporting its member organisations and representing their interests to the government. In a similar way, Volunteering England supports and advises individual volunteer centres and organisations around the country, although it also provides information and ideas for individual volunteers.

Word of mouth is perhaps the most effective endorsement an organisation can get, so ask your work colleagues, friends or acquaintances if they have ever volunteered or could recommend a charity to you. You may find that the person you've been sitting opposite at work has been fundraising for the RSPB for years and you've never known it.

Local versus national organisations

Deciding which voluntary organisation to give your time to may be made slightly easier if you think about whether you want to work for a local branch of a national organisation, or for a smaller concern close to home. This decision may be taken out of your hands if, for example, you're interested in working with animals but the only organisation involved in this work locally is a national charity, or if you want to support local heritage and the only site near you is a National Trust property.

There are pros and cons for volunteering for both small and large organisations. Larger charities are more likely to have dedicated volunteer managers, so the process of starting volunteering should be smoother and any problems that may arise may be handled better because there will be systems in place to deal with them. With bigger budgets, these organisations have more money to invest in their volunteers, so you may get more training opportunities, which could be important if you see volunteering as a step towards a career change.

However, it is easy to feel lost in a big organisation and if you want to feel you are touching the lives of people in your own community, opting for a smaller organisation near home may be more suitable. Smaller organisations can be just as efficient as the larger ones, because they will have fewer people to manage, and if there is less money for training, what you do get may be more specialised. With a smaller organisation you could get more hands-on experience and find you are given more responsibility more quickly because there are fewer people to do the work.

In the end, the choice of which organisation you volunteer for should be driven by the kind of volunteering you want to do.

Whatever charity you choose to get involved with, you need to know that you can trust it. When an organisation says it is supporting the work of small farmers in Angola, how can you check that those farmers are really getting help? And if a voluntary group claims to be providing quality meals for local elderly residents, how do you know they are not being given lower-cost options?

It is important you feel comfortable with the work and ethics of your chosen charity, otherwise you could soon find yourself disillusioned and let down.

Find out as much as you can about the organisation before you start. Read up on its origins and its mission statement. Again, try to contact past and current volunteers to gauge opinion and even try to speak to paid staff. It might be worth checking with your local volunteer centre to see if they have heard any good or bad reviews. A quick search online could also produce some interesting results. You may find someone has blogged about the charity or it is listed on a website dedicated to exposing rogue organisations.

The Charity Commission, the independent regulator of charities in England and Wales, keeps a register of legitimate organisations, which can be searched online. This could prove useful to see what it says about the one you have chosen, although many community groups will not be registered as charities.

Finding out about the credentials of an organisation that sends volunteers overseas can be trickier. The best advice is to volunteer through a high-profile organisation, such as VSO, which has a good reputation in the sector.

When to say no

The aims and ideals of the majority of volunteering organisations are to help people and communities in need. However, there are cases where volunteers can make a bad situation worse. This is something you should be particularly aware of if you want to head overseas.

If you want to feel that you are making a long-term difference to a community, then you need to think about whether your short-term efforts are going to be sustainable. The point of volunteering in a developing country is to assist, not to take over. So if you are going to spend a year teaching in a village school in Tanzania, you need to be sure that you are not taking that job away from a local teacher. If you are going abroad to teach English without a specialist qualification, think about whether you will really be able to offer a good service to your pupils. Instead of heading abroad now, it might be worth building up your skills here for a year or two so you have something worthwhile to contribute when you do eventually go overseas.

Think about how you can share your knowledge and experience with local people, so they can do the work on their own once you leave.

A good way of finding out about the sustainability of your commitment is to look at what your chosen charity has achieved over the past five or ten years. What progress has it made towards achieving its aims?

Finding your place

Once you've narrowed down your search, it is time to find out how you go about volunteering.

Most charities and NGOs, unless they are very small, will have their own website, which can be used not only to discover its aims and ambitions, but also to apply for a post.

Unless you're applying for a specifically advertised voluntary post, you will probably need to register an interest by filling in your contact details, the type of volunteering you'd like to do, and your availability. You may also be asked if you have a driving licence.

If you don't have one specific organisation that you wish to work with, get in touch with timebank.org.uk or do-it.org.uk. TimeBank runs all sort of innovative projects, both on its own and in partnership with other charities. If none of those suit your current situation they will take information about your skills and interests, either over the phone or through their website, and work with Volunteer Centres to match you to suitable opportunities. Do-It operates an online database; you enter your area of interest, the type of activity you wish to do and where you live and you will then be offered a list of possible opportunities. You can apply online and your application goes directly to the charity, which will then get in touch. If you are applying for a role that involves working with children or young people, you will probably be called for an interview before being accepted.

Checklist

Before getting in touch with any charity, consider the following:

☐ The aim of an organisation

Most will have a statement of intent or belief. Make sure you support what the organisation stands for and believes in. If it is a religious organisation, you may be required to sign a declaration of belief. If it is a campaigning charity, make sure you feel comfortable with its goals.

☐ The work you will undertake

Having a clear understanding of what you will be asked to do is crucial. It helps you to decide if the work is really what you had in mind when you first thought about giving your time. Consider if you are physically and emotionally suited to the opportunity, as you may find yourself working with people who are terminally ill or going through difficult periods of their lives. Try to think about the work you will be doing in the long term. Is there any chance that you could lose interest within a few weeks?

☐ Training and qualifications

In many organisations, some initial training will be necessary, if for no other reason than to familiarise you with how they operate. If you will need to undertake more structural training, ask how long this will take, where it will be held and what it involves. If you are interested in gaining a qualification, make this clear at the outset. This way the training could be tailored to suit your goal.

☐ Payment

Most organisations cover reasonable out-of-pocket expenses, but never assume this is the case, so always ask. Receiving expenses should not affect the payment of welfare benefits (see page 19)

☐ Supervision

It is worth finding out how much supervision you will get before you begin, as some people who don't feel confident working on their own may require a lot of support, while others are far happier working independently. Ask about supervision if you feel it will affect your enjoyment of your voluntary work.

☐ **Where you will be working**

There's no point working in a place you don't like. Be honest. If you've always wanted to work outdoors with your local sports club, then make sure you're not stuck behind a desk managing the finances. Equally, if you want to support a local conservation group by advertising their work to the community, make it clear that you won't be spending Saturday mornings at the park with a spade in your hand.

☐ **Insurance**

If you are working with vulnerable people or if you are using specialist equipment, it is important that the organisation's insurance covers you. Check that you will be fully insured under its policy. Read more about volunteering and the law in Chapter seven.

☐ **References and police checks**

Criminal record checks are required of anyone working with children and vulnerable adults (see page 20). These can take some time to process, so only consider joining organisations involved in working with these groups if you are in it for the long haul. You may be asked to provide a reference, perhaps from someone who has known you for a long time or from an employer to give the organisation an idea of your character and how you cope under pressure. Not all organisations will do this, so ask before you apply if it is a concern.

☐ **Sitting an interview**

Some organisations will want to have an informal chat to find out a bit more about you, such as how you heard about the opportunities available, why you want to get involved, if you have any special needs, and if you are prepared to undergo training. If you want to work with children and vulnerable adults you are more likely to be asked to sit an interview. Of course, this process is not a one-way thing. An interview will give you the chance to ask questions and get a feel of what it might be like to work for your chosen organisation.

6. Striking a balance

From volunteering at work to volunteering in your pyjamas, there are many ways of incorporating volunteering into your everyday life. The most important thing is that volunteering fits in with your lifestyle and time commitments. This chapter suggests some ways that you can integrate volunteering into your life without it eating too much into your own time.

Employee schemes

Times have changed in the workplace. Where once the voluntary efforts of a company may have amounted to a collecting tin in left reception for a local charity, there is a growing awareness among businesses that getting more involved with the voluntary sector through partnerships improves the skills of its workforce and can enhance its public image.

More businesses are starting to offer their workers the chance to volunteer through company projects, such as running a mentoring scheme at a local school - which can be fitted in during lunchtime or at the beginning of the day - or one-off 'challenge events', such as refurbishing a youth club or spending an evening helping to tidy a communal area outside the office. These schemes are known as employer supported volunteering (ESV).

The number of employers getting involved in ESV is rising. By 2003, 74 per cent of the FTSE Top 100 companies had some kind of employer volunteering programme, and around 1.5 million employees were actively involved.

Basically, ESV brings a third party into the volunteering equation - the employer. A company can supply a volunteering organisation with a group of willing volunteers with valuable skills and experience. These schemes also help to forge closer links between the public and private sectors. They take the pressure off people with full-time jobs who want to volunteer, but who feel they haven't got the time outside the working day to dedicate to a project.

How ESV schemes work

How ESV schemes work varies from one organisation to another. Some employers offer paid time off to volunteer up to a specified number of hours per month or per year, others offer employees time off in lieu or allow them to have more flexible working hours so they can fit in volunteering during the working day. In 2005 alone, almost a quarter of employees in England and Wales received paid time off to volunteer on ESV schemes.

By joining your employer's scheme, you will get the chance to develop new skills in a completely new environment. You may be able to work with other people in the company who you have not met before. It can also enhance your future job prospects. More than half of the top 200 companies surveyed by Reed Executive said voluntary work can be more valuable than experience gained in paid employment.

If you are thinking of trying to persuade your employer of the benefits of ESV, it might be worth pointing out that it could improve the credibility of your organisation, provide training opportunities for staff and generally boost morale. ESV schemes are also part of the government's wider agenda on voluntary action and civil renewal, which aims to inspire people to make a difference in their communities. Ministers see corporate involvement as one of the keys to its success. A business that is involved in volunteering shows the government that it is playing an active part in its community and will no doubt improve its standing in the eyes of local officials.

The choice is yours

According to a survey carried out by Community Service Volunteers (CSV) during their 2006 Make A Difference Day campaign, the most popular form of volunteering among the workforce was with young people, with 39 per cent of volunteers saying they wanted to help youngsters improve their numeracy skills and career options or take part in a mentoring scheme. Work to improve the environment was also popular with 35 per cent of employees. However, only 3 per cent said they wanted to work in hospitals and 8 per cent with homeless people or the elderly.

If your company doesn't support employee volunteering, why not think about setting up a scheme in your own firm? You can get a wealth of advice from Employees in the Community Network, Business in the Community and the CSV.

PHOEBE FRICKER, 26, is an advertising services executive for a national newspaper. She teaches reading at a local school during her lunch hour.

I volunteer through CSV at work. It was just something I was interested in and I knew I could do it in my lunch hour. There are lots of immigrant children in the King's Cross area in London who need extra help because English is their second language. They especially need one-on-one tuition because they don't get very much of that at school.

The first time was scary and quite nerve-racking. Hilda, who is originally from Ghana and is eight years old, could barely understand me. I remember thinking: 'Oh no, this is awful. This is terrible. it is not going to work.' But by the second week she'd already made great improvements. It seemed that as soon as she realised that I was going to keep coming back, that this wasn't a one-off, she began to trust me. To begin with she'd barely answered my questions but now she'll volunteer

information. She's really opened up and it is amazing.

Hilda and I start off by reading a book and then we might play a game or chat - anything that helps her to practise her English and get more confident.

It is great that I can do it through work. My boss has told me that whatever time I need I can have it. There was an afternoon of training at the beginning and he was understanding about it. In the meantime because it is in a lunch hour I don't feel under lots of pressure. It is easy to slip back into work mode afterwards.

Hilda is lovely - cheerful and chatty and smiley. It is amazing what you can achieve in just one hour a week. It is not a lot to give but it makes a big difference.

Virtual Volunteering

With most people having access to a computer and the internet, you can now volunteer in this country or internationally without having to take your slippers off.

Virtual volunteering means making a contribution to society via the internet, on site or on your home PC. This could be through translation work, monitoring online chat boards, or perhaps, if you're a mentor, keeping in touch with a mentee between sessions.

This virtual approach is ideal if you want to voluntee but are unable, or unwilling, to do so in person, perhaps because of family responsibilities, time commitments or illness. Not only does the virtual route allow more people to participate, it could also make volunteering much more convenient for existing volunteers. Here are some ideas for using your virtual skills.

- Sharing your expertise: This could involve answering legal or financial questions that have been posted on an online advice forum, writing computer programs, or designing a marketing strategy or website.
- Online research: You could source information from the internet for a charity's newsletter or website, put together a grant proposal, update the contact details of fellow volunteers or those of the organisation, or simply keep up to date with issues relating to your organisation's cause, particularly regarding new pieces of legislation.
- Writing and editing: An organisation always needs to get its message out, so if you have the skills perhaps you could source information and write articles, proofread other people's copy, or edit publications.
- Translating: If your charity of choice is involved in helping people overseas, then translating legal documents or other texts could be perfect for linguists.
- Designing: An organisation will always need help in publishing brochures or leaflets. If you've an eye for design, perhaps you could help to create a new logo or poster, or even design a website.
- Provide IT services: Think about preparing a PowerPoint or other computer-based presentation to help out a member of your organisation's staff. Perhaps you could

set up a video-conference or register an organisation's webpage with search engines and blogs.

- Managing and mentoring: Any online discussion forums will need monitoring, so consider volunteering to supervise a chat room once or twice a week. Perhaps you could offer free online tuition, or input volunteering opportunities into online databases. If you want to get involved in mentoring, it doesn't have to be done face to face. You could keep in regular contact through email.
- Make contact: This could mean staying in touch online with a housebound person, or supporting someone who is finding it difficult working overseas. It could also involve keeping other volunteers on your rota up to date with news and events.

Managing yourself

While you will have the joy of flexibility, you will still need to find time during your day to do the work. It could be easy to take on more work than you can handle because you know you can do it from your kitchen table at 2 a.m. So it is important you learn how to manage your time and know what you're getting into.

- Make sure you are clear about what you are expected to do. If the job description is unclear and you can't find the appropriate information on the organisation's website, don't be afraid to ask.
- Keep in regular contact with your organisation; make sure it keeps you up to date with any new developments that could affect your work.
- Your organisation will probably have policies and set procedures regarding confidentiality or how to represent it in public, for example. Make sure you stick to them.
- Pace yourself. You may not follow the same routine at home as you would in the office and it could be easy to overdo it. Take breaks from your computer to avoid headaches and eyestrain.
- Draw up a timetable to help you organise your time. It can be easy to let the days slide by without doing anything and suddenly find yourself facing a looming deadline.
- Don't over-commit your time. It can be tempting to take on too much at first. Start with a small project and see how you go.
- Finally, recognise if an arrangement isn't working and take steps to change it.

Getting Started

Because this is still a relatively new area of volunteering, some smaller organisations may not have tapped into it yet, so you may need to convince them of its merits. This shouldn't be too difficult as using the internet could dramatically cut an organisation's expenses, an ever-present obstacle to a lot of volunteering programmes.

Not-for-profit organisations are waking up to the possibilities of the internet to recruit and train volunteers, share resources and communicate instantly - without increasing spending. it is not unfeasible that many of an organisation's jobs could be done via the internet. So if your chosen organisation does not currently offer virtual volunteering as a way to contribute, consider helping them to make this an option.

The idea behind virtual volunteering is that it streamlines, facilitates and supports what a group already offers, so don't attempt to introduce new services if they can't be delivered. You're not trying to replace old-fashioned face-to-face communication with a computer screen; that can never be replaced, but this could be a way of improving what you do.

Make good use of email

Email can be far more convenient than using the telephone. Many people feel they can be more assertive and direct when they are not talking face to face. They can also be more forthcoming with ideas or find it easier to say no. And as emails are documented proof of a conversation, people may take more care to check their facts before they share their thoughts.

Sending information via email, rather than in paper form, not only helps to save the planet, but is also cheaper, more direct and more efficient. Emailing reminders, updates and feedback works better than a traditional noticeboard for getting the message out.

Email lists (and online discussion groups) provide opportunities for people to share thoughts and advice, make communication widely accessible and promote collaboration.

Offer in-house training

Virtual volunteering is still a relatively new phenomenon in the UK, and the internet may be new territory for people within your organisation. Offering training in this field could open up new opportunities for people, particularly those who are thinking of giving up volunteering because they are unable to dedicate a two-hour block of time on a Friday night.

Amend policies

If your organisation has written policies relating to volunteers, they may need updating to incorporate the issues surrounding virtual volunteering. This might include how to claim expenses when you're not leaving your home. Who better to think about the issues than someone already involved in virtual volunteering?

Stay on the look-out

Look at how other organisations use the internet to support the services they offer - they could be applicable to you.

Residential volunteering

If you feel like getting away from it all, then this could be just the thing for you. Residential volunteering is like a working holiday, but more fun and tremendously rewarding. Dedicating perhaps a week, a month, or even a year to a voluntary project means that not only will you more readily see the fruits of your labour, you will also get a real feel for the people, or place, you are wanting to help.

While some people may associate residential volunteering with overseas work, there are many organisations in the UK that offer opportunities that can be fitted into your work or school holidays.

This type of volunteering is open to all ages, with some organisations accepting people from 16. And it is a great way to make a difference if you are claiming benefits. Volunteers living away from home can still receive housing and council tax benefit and income support for housing costs for up to 13 weeks.

One thing to watch out for is the cost. While some UK organisations may pay your expenses, others may not. If not, the cost to you shouldn't be too high (especially compared with what you would pay for a two-week volunteering trip abroad), and will probably be for accommodation and food. Remember, though, the accommodation is unlikely to be a five-star hotel, so if after a day toiling on the land you want to soak in a warm bath in your en-suite room with a drink from the mini-bar, you might want to make your own sleeping arrangements.

Most residential placements in the UK are geared towards environmental, social care or animal welfare projects.

Environmental work

Those interested in the environment and heritage could take up a one-week or weekend voluntary trip with the National Trust at one of its properties. The trust runs more than 400 working holidays each year, from herding goats to painting a lighthouse. Costs are around £65 for a week, which includes meals and accommodation. You have to be over 18 to join one of these teams, which can be of mixed or similar age ranges, and you will need to be in relatively good physical health as the work can be quite demanding.

The trust has specific youth discovery residential projects for those between the ages of 16 and 18.

The National Trust's Active Holidays are slightly different, offering you the chance to combine countryside conservation work with outdoor pursuits such as pony trekking, canoeing or sailing. Some of these holidays are run in association with the John Muir Trust, which means you will spend two days and one evening exploring the local landscape and will leave with a nationally recognised John Muir Explorer award.

The National Trust has longer-term residential projects, ranging from three months to a year. It also runs open-air theatre and music events, which require volunteers to help to set up beforehand and clear up afterwards.

Animal welfare work

If you are interested in birds and wildlife, spending some time on one of the RSPB's reserves working as a warden could be ideal. The work you will do varies from season to season, but could include tree planting, leading guided walks or farm work. Placements can be up to six months and volunteers have to be over 16.

Social care opportunities

CSV (Community Service Volunteers) is one of the more high-profile bodies that offer full-time placements of between four and twelve months in more than 1,000 projects in the UK. These are open to anyone between the ages of 16 and 35. The work is usually in a caring capacity, perhaps helping someone with disabilities to live independently or attend university, helping in a day centre or night shelter for the homeless, or with a family that needs help coping with a child who has a specific illness or disability. The CSV pays pocket money, travel expenses, accommodation and food.

Other opportunities in this field include joining the Independent Living Alternatives organisation, whose volunteers work in partnerships with people with disabilities who require physical support. Volunteers need to be at least 18 and have at least four months to spare. Accommodation, food, travel expenses and any other additional expenses will be paid, and volunteers will receive pocket money and training.

Vitalise, formerly the Winged Fellowship Trust, provides holidays for visually impaired and people with disabilities, and residential volunteers have the option of providing practical support, perhaps as a sighted guide, or spending a couple of weeks working at one of its centres around the country, catering for people with physical disabilities. Food and accommodation are provided and travel expenses up to an agreed limit are reimbursed.

Some children's charities also offer residential projects, such as summer camps, for young people, which provide respite care for parents of children with disabilities.

Responding to a crisis

Within hours of the south-east Asian tsunami on 26 December 2004, news and images of the scale of destruction and the loss of life were flashed around the globe. While the public was getting to grips with what it saw, charities and NGOs were assessing the practical needs of the survivors in those devastated areas and putting into practice the rapid response strategies they have developed for this kind of humanitarian emergency. And for that they need a band of skilled workers, such as public health educators, engineers, project managers and logistics experts, who can be called on at short notice.

While this is not strictly volunteering, if you are interested in this sort of work, you can contact relief and development organisations such as the British Red Cross, Oxfam or Tearfund to register an interest. If your skills meet the requirements, you will be sent for basic training in what you will be expected to do overseas, and what you can expect when you arrive at a disaster zone. If you are accepted as an emergency worker, you will be placed on a call-out rota. You could be on call for a month at a time, during which you will need to be prepared to head overseas at a moment's notice. Unless you have a very understanding employer, you will probably have to take this time off as unpaid leave. However, most aid organisations will pay you market rates for the type of work you will be doing.

At times of crisis and natural disaster, many people without the above key skills will feel a compulsion to get involved, but before you rush to buy a ticket for the next plane to an affected zone, stop and think about what you will actually be contributing. A desire to help is great, but in times of major catastrophes like the 2004 tsunami, it needs to be coupled with appropriate experience. Get in touch with a relief organisation to see what help is required and how you can use your gifts to help closer to home.

After the tsunami, some charities complained that the number of well-meaning people heading to Thailand and Sri Lanka was counter-productive and that they actually hindered the work being carried out. Not only is that bad news for the people who you are trying to help, but it could be discouraging for you. If you contact an organisation first, at least you will know that however you contribute you are making a difference, which is why you wanted to get involved in the first place.

Family volunteering

If you're a parent who is juggling work, looking after children, cooking, cleaning and trying to snatch a moment or two with friends, volunteering may seem just too much of an effort. Where are you going to find the time? And if you do find the odd hour or two in an average week, will that mean you neglect something, or someone, else you consider important?

If these are concerns of yours, you could always consider volunteering as a family. Not only will it mean you get to spend some quality time together on a regular basis - something that can be hard to squeeze out of life's hectic schedule - but you'll also be able to achieve something worthwhile for your community.

As a family, you could find that sharing a meaningful experience will bring you closer together. Perhaps you will see each other in a new light, and develop a newfound respect for each other.

It is never too early to start volunteering, and in the same way that it can help adults to develop new skills and increase their social circle, it can improve a child's confidence, make them more aware of the world around them and help them to make friends. It could also encourage them to become more tolerant and cooperative, improve their communication skills and may be more meaningful than putting money in a collection box. And, of course, people who volunteer as children are likely to grow up to become volunteering adults. Children are renowned for their boundless energy, and can often be more enthusiastic, imaginative and energetic than older people, so why not try to channel all this into something positive?

But family volunteering doesn't have to mean just getting your immediate family involved. Why not ask nephews and nieces, cousins, grandchildren and grandparents to join in? Not only will this be good news for your chosen organisation, which will have several new pairs of helping hands, it also means if you can't find time to volunteer one week, your absence won't be missed in quite the same way as if you were volunteering alone, as there will still be plenty of people to help.

Deciding what to do

Choosing the right activity and organisation is important if you want the whole family to stay excited and enthusiastic, so careful planning and thought will be needed.

Make sure everyone is involved in the decision-making, so no one feels excluded. Find out what everyone is interested in. Is your daughter passionate about the environment? Is your son interested in sports? Does your partner want to work with animals? It might not be easy coming to a decision, but try to find common ground so that all the family are happy. Possible family activities include getting involved in programmes for children and young people, school or sports activities, environmental projects or helping older people.

The skills needed for a volunteering opportunity will also be a consideration. Do you all have the specific requirements? Are you all strong enough to pull up weeds or patient enough to spend time with people with disabilities? Try to choose a goal-orientated activity that accomplishes a lot in a short space of time. This will keep children interested and dedicated for longer.

Although some volunteering activities are not designed with very young children in mind, this type of family volunteering is starting to become more commonplace.

How long have you got?

This is a crucial question. Some families may find time to help at an after-school activity once a week or once a month, while others may only have Saturday mornings or Sunday afternoons to spare. If regular weekday slots are hard to come by, then consider doing something rewarding in the school holidays.

If nothing appeals, why not set up your own project? That way you can fit it in when you want and tailor it to your family requirements. See page 71 for more on doing it yourself.

If you haven't time to go out and about, how about putting together a resource and supply pack of paper and pens for a school in a developing country, or researching information together? Or how about collectively writing to a family overseas?

If you can give an hour or two once a week or once a month, think about serving meals at a local homeless shelter, or working on an environmental project. Maybe you and your children could befriend someone in a nursing home. Suggest starting a newsletter for your street, as a way of fostering community spirit. It could include stories, poems, pictures and local news. Contact your local council to see if you could help organise an event that allows children to paint a mural in a public place, or plant trees in their playground.

Safety

Safety is still an issue when you're working as a team, especially when you are working with children, so make sure you:

- Stay informed - make sure you are aware of any safety concerns that are specific to your project.
- Listen carefully - make sure you follow directions and make sure no one in your family is confused by instructions. Don't be afraid to ask.
- Use caution - make sure children know that it is fine to say no if something does not seem right.
- Stay together - let your children know that you will be nearby.

Volunteering should be something your family remembers as a fun learning experience. Reflect on what you've learned individually and collectively, or what you might do differently next time. Prompt your children to talk about what they enjoyed about their volunteering project. Emphasise what you have achieved or the difference you might have made. You could make a scrapbook of your work, or a poster with photos as something to remember the experience. You never know, volunteering could become an important family ritual.

Providing parental support

If you're not sure you can rally your family to volunteer, they can still play their part in helping you to get involved. Real Parents is a campaign run by TimeBank in partnership with Home-Start which is a support charity for families that need extra help. The only requirement for being a volunteer with these charities is having a family of your own. The idea is that you can draw on your own experiences of raising a family to support another family under pressure, perhaps because of post-natal depression, disabilities, bereavement, multiple births, or parents who are very young and have no support networks of their own. Just having the support of someone who has been there before can offer comfort to a person feeling overwhelmed by parenthood.

Volunteering for this organisation involves visiting a family for a couple of hours each week. As needs vary, so do the types of support required. You might be providing practical assistance, helping to clean up round the house, or simply offering company for a single mother who is desperate for another adult to talk to.

Do it yourself

Sometimes if you want a job done, you have to roll up your sleeves and do it yourself. So, if you look around your community and see a need that is not being met - perhaps there's not enough to keep young people occupied, or asylum seekers aren't getting the support they need - then think about organising your own group to do something about it. More and more people are beginning to get involved in voluntary work in this way. Establishing your own voluntary group doesn't mean you will have to apply for official charitable status. In fact, the guidelines on what constitutes a charity are becoming more stringent. Contact the Charity Commission for the latest advice.

Setting up your own organisation will take a lot of time and commitment, so think carefully before you take the plunge, but remember that enthusiasm and the conviction that what you are doing is right will carry you a long way. And the sense of achievement you will feel when you see the results will be worth all the effort.

KATE REW, a 37-year-old freelance journalist, set up the Outdoor Swimming Society which raises money for research into breast cancer.

My mother was told she had breast cancer in 1991. In a way she was lucky - she was able to take part in trials for a new drug called Tamoxifen, and she survived. Fifteen years later she is alive and well but ever since she was diagnosed I've felt that there was some sort of karmic debt to pay in a way. We don't know for definite if it is the drugs which have kept her healthy but I wanted to put something back into cancer research.

At the same time I've always loved outdoor swimming and felt that we've become estranged from our rivers and lidos. People have become scared of swimming outside since the invention of chlorinated pools. Yet whether you're floating downstream looking at the clouds or striking out across a remote lake, swimming outdoors is one of life's true pleasures. The world looks brighter after an open-air swim, as if, while you were out there, someone coloured it in.

These two passions came together when I decided to set up the Outdoor Swimming Society. At first I wasn't sure how to get started - whether to take a step back from work for a year and set the whole thing up gradually or do it on the hoof. In the end we chose the second option and I'm so glad we did. I found an advertising agency who took the whole concept on as their pet project and donated their services for free; an event management company that knows how to organise big occasions; and a swimming professional who could give advice. Everyone who is involved had been touched by breast cancer in some way and became committed to the whole idea. It has been like that all along - born out of people's passion both for supporting breast cancer and loving the water.

It has amazed me how it is taken off. Over the year we raised £70,000 by holding sponsored swims outdoors, which was fantastic. It has made me realise people just need the confidence to put their ideas out there. Anything can happen - there is a sea of goodwill and enthusiasm. People really will do bonkers things if you touch their imaginations.

I'm always looking for volunteers. At the moment we particularly need canoeists, lifeguards, administration people, legal advisers and accountants. In 2007 we're planning something called 'The Big Jump' in July. It is part of a European-wide campaign to get rivers cleaned up. In France they have over 1,000 rivers where it is safe to swim; in this country there are only 11. I always tell people - I've never had a bad outside swim. Swimming outdoors just makes you feel happy. There's something amazing about being at the same level as the lilies and the ducks. You can float with the current and forget about normal life for a while.

You're not alone

If you've spotted that something needs to be done in your community, then others probably have as well, so start asking around, telling people what you're thinking of doing to spark interest. Do your research and you might discover there is an existing group already carrying out the work you are interested in. A merger could mean accomplishing more than if you carry on working alone.

It might be useful to speak to your local National Association for Voluntary and Community Action (www.navca.org.uk), which might be able to offer you help or advice, and you should also try your local authority, which may be able to put you in touch with relevant officers or community workers. Your local authority is unlikely to offer you any money for your project, but it should be able to advise you on other funding options. Do some research to see if there are any related associations that may offer guidance, or a national charity that might have local contacts.

There are also organisations that support social entrepreneurs, such as the Community Action Network (www.can-online.org.uk), which may be able to offer advice and support. Your local Citizens' Advice Bureau might be another source of help. You can find the nearest branch on its website (www.citizensadvice.org.uk).

If you want to take things a step further, the School for Social Entrepreneurs offers training for anyone who wants to use their entrepreneurial abilities in the not-for-profit arena. If you're a young person who wants to do your own thing, the scheme Millennium Volunteers helps 16 to 24-year-olds set up their own projects.

When you've gathered together a group of like-minded people, or are comfortable going it alone, then it is time to consider the essentials of setting up your project.

Getting organised

Excessive meetings and bureaucracy can quickly dampen the enthusiasm of the most passionate volunteer, so while some paperwork and discussions will be needed, try to keep them to a minimum.

Start off with one or two informal meetings to establish what skills and, crucially, how much time the group has to give to the project. Define the purpose of what you are doing and the roles individuals will play. And think of a name for your organisation. It might be a good idea to take notes, just so that everyone knows where they stand.

Even if you are not setting up an official charity, it might be helpful to establish a few rules, such as how decisions will be made - will a management committee be created to make decisions or will the entire group be involved? Who will sit on any committee and how will they be elected? Who will take minutes of meetings, or keep financial records?

Once these ground rules are established it will make the actual job of raising money and promoting awareness of your cause much easier. The key thing is to appoint the right people to the right jobs - and appreciate that no one person's job is any more important than anyone else's. For every person with all the headline-grabbing fundraising ideas, there will be a diligent treasurer managing any outgoing costs and calculating the profits.

Get the message out

Once you've established the ground rules, you can begin to publicise your group. The more you get the message out about what you are trying to achieve, the more people will want to get involved, either by donating money or through practical help.

Think about what you want to achieve through your publicity. Are you trying to attract more members to your group and raise money, or advertise what you are doing for the people who will ultimately benefit from your work?

There are a number of ways to spread the word of your endeavours, and all could be worth a try. Think about publishing a newsletter, which sets out your aims and what activities you will be doing over the coming weeks or months. This can be handed out at other related community events or to people in the street, or a pile could be left in the local library.

Create posters and leaflets and get them pasted up around your area and delivered door to door. Contact your local paper or radio station, either to advertise your work or to publicise coming events. Think about how you can make all you do eye-catching - you are more likely to attract people's attention if you have an interesting name or logo.

A word of warning: there is such a thing as bad publicity. The golden rule is: if you tell people you are going to put on a jumble sale, collect money outside the local supermarket, or respond to emails or telephone calls, then you have to do it. Unless there is a very good reason for you not doing these things, a cancelled event or a call that was not returned will make you seem unprofessional, and if you're perceived to be unreliable in one area, people could question your abilities to manage funds or do the other work you claim to be involved in. The best way of avoiding these situations is not to take on too much too soon. Don't organise five events and promise three newsletters every month if you haven't the manpower to do it. Your long-term achievement will be greater if you start off small and build the organisation up slowly.

Getting funding

Raising enough money to allow you to achieve all your aims is never going to be easy - but persevere and be inventive.

It is not just about getting hold of the cash. Some people or businesses can offer other vital commodities, such as prizes for competitions or a venue for a function. Contact local businesses, trusts and foundations to see if they will help with financial support or gifts in kind. Use your contacts, and call in favours - if anyone has ever said they would help you out, now is the time to take them up on their offer. The wider your network of helpers, the more chance you have of achieving results.

If you are fundraising, be clear about where the money is going - will it help to meet set-up costs, or go directly towards those in need? Nothing puts people off giving more than lack of clarity. Keep in mind that people may be more compelled to give their money or time if they know it will directly benefit the person or group you are trying to help, rather than being swallowed up in administration costs.

Put on events. Not only will they raise funds, they will raise the profile of your organisation. Think of events that are media-friendly. A jumble sale is a solid, relatively easy way of raising money, but a sponsored abseil down a building in your town centre will bring in more cash and has more chance of getting a local reporter along, even if it takes a little more thought and planning.

Make sure you keep records of where your money comes from and how it is spent, no matter how small the sum. It is simple to do: just keep a notebook listing your income and expenses on separate pages. Keep receipts for everything. This way, not only will you and the committee know where you stand financially, you will be able to demonstrate more clearly to others what you are doing and what you have achieved.

Throughout the whole process, the important thing to keep at the forefront of your mind is why you set up the group in the first place. Knowing you will help to improve someone's life or the local environment will help you get through the long committee meetings and the occasional sleepless night.

NICK STANHOPE, 26, organised a cycle ride from Cape Town in South Africa to London to raise money and awareness of the charity Anti-Slavery International. He is the author of the book Blood, Sweat and Charity.

At university I was involved in human rights issues, campaigning and raising money for Amnesty International. But listening to a talk by Kevin Bales, who wrote *Disposable People: New Slavery in the Global Economy*, motivated me to get involved in the anti-slavery movement. I decided I wanted to do something big to

raise money, so I planned a cycling trip from Cape Town to London, to raise money for Anti-Slavery International, making a documentary about the state of modern slavery in the countries we travelled through and then doing campaigning and awareness-raising among schools when we came back.

We graduated from university in 2002 and five of us started the cycle in August 2003. It took six and a half months. It was hard, but amazing. We were really lucky because we got to meet people affected by slavery. We cycled 80 to 100 miles a day. When we got back we did 50 talks around the UK. So I volunteered for about 18 months on top of other part-time work, and since then I've carried on doing bits and pieces.

There is a huge amount of organisation to a trip like this. It took a year to set up and fundraise for, so I found a teaching job that gave me the time to take the bulk of this on. Within the group we allocated roles in areas that we knew something about. For example, someone plotted the logistics of our trip - visas, access to money, health considerations; while I sorted out the technical aspects - equipment and training.

We spent a lot of time accumulating contacts that could help us with every need we had. These ranged from people providing alcohol for fundraising events, to discounts for bikes, to people to stay with in each country, to people to train us in documentary-making. This was vital and the help we got was incredible. We worked hard to make everyone feel part of the trip, kept them updated on progress, invited them to events and sent them a copy of the film we made.

We became mini-experts in the issue of modern slavery in a broad sense and in all the countries we went through - this made us much more effective campaigners. Through fundraising events, awareness presentations, film screenings and my book signings, we probably raised awareness among about 5,000 people. For an issue that most people think has been consigned to history, this was really valuable. We were able to set up some long-term relationships between our supporters and Anti-Slavery International that will benefit them for years to come.

Fundraising is probably the most difficult process. People want to know that you are passionate and professional and you believe strongly in what you are doing. I believe they will give money to the people doing the project, not the cause or social trends. Some people make the mistake of talking about the social impact of the cause without talking about themselves or the people affected by it. It is just as valuable, though, when people give their time and skills and contacts, rather than money.

We were very careful about money. Personally I think that people should never have to make a contribution to support you that is being split between the charity and expenses. Either you cover all expenses yourself or raise money from family and close friends specifically to cover costs - and say upfront that this is where the money is going. You can then approach everyone else with the assurance that all money goes to charity, which will make them happier to support you and more generous, and their donation will be able to benefit from Gift Aid.

The total money involved for this trip was about £60,000 - £40,000 raised for Anti-Slavery, £10,000 raised specifically towards costs and £10,000 from our own funds. Of the money that we used for expenses, we did two things: we gave ourselves a small daily stipend, based upon what a local campaigner would get to sustain themselves; and we bought things that could be sold on return to the UK, such as bikes and equipment. Any other expense over the six months was from our own funds. Probably 50 per cent of our expenses (equipment, health care, etc.) were sponsored through gifts in kind. Anti-Slavery were very happy with the way we approached it and we always had a clear answer when we were questioned on this - which is quite a contentious issue.

Anti-Slavery are a small organisation and didn't have as much time as they would have liked to help us, but they were great and we had a very good relationship with them, which is still strong.

I would recommend that people think carefully about what they will need from charities and lay it out upfront. The charity will not have scheduled to support the challenge, unless it is planned a long way in advance, so everything they do for you will be extra. Some charities are better at dealing with this than others, of course.

We've kept links going with Anti-Slavery and will probably stay in contact with that charity forever. I hope to become a trustee in the long term.

Volunteering through the seasons

January

With post-Christmas and pre-payday blues, January finds many of us at a low ebb. New Year resolutions have been broken, the weather's terrible and lots of people may need something to help restore some festive cheer. What could be more uplifting than kittens? Help to shoulder the burden of your local pet shelter by fostering kittens, puppies or other animals.

February

If you find yourself without a Valentine's day card, don't bother with speed dating, personal columns or dating agencies. Volunteering is a great way to meet new people with shared interests. Whether or not you're on your own in February, help someone to escape their isolation by lending a listening ear with Samaritans.

March

Spring is just around the corner, the time of year when many of us are thinking about having a good clearout. But why limit your spring-cleaning to taking unwanted belongings to a charity shop? This is a great time to dig out brooms, brushes and buckets to work on refurbishing and restoring public spaces. Get outdoors and help to make your local area a better place by collecting rubbish, planting flowers and covering up graffiti.

April

The London Marathon takes place in April and in 2005 more than 30,000 people took part, a significant number running for charity. However, if you haven't got a place this year, why not consider stewarding the event? You'd still be doing your bit, without the months of training.

May

Feeling passionate about social and political issues on May Day? Spend some time during the May bank holiday campaigning for your cause. Have your say: write a letter to your MP, draw up a petition or visit the website PowerToThePeople.org.uk for more ideas.

June

As June sees the longest day of the year, many people have more energy and feel more inclined get involved and make things happen. Summer is also a great time for a party. Why not get people in your road together and organise a street party for charity?

July

Go to a music festival for free by working as a festival steward. Oxfam runs three-shift schemes where you can help out by checking tickets and passes, monitoring campsites, keeping an eye on overcrowding and picking up litter. You also get to watch the bands.

August

It is summer and time for a holiday. This is an opportunity to volunteer with an organisation that runs holidays for people with disabilities, such as Vitalise. Volunteers help people relax and have fun, and provide respite for carers.

September

During September many children are consumed by back-to-school anxieties. Whether their problem is homework or PE teachers, you can support someone through the ordeals of school by becoming a mentor.

October

If you're too old for trick-or-treating, celebrate Halloween by donating blood to The National Blood Service.

November

Bonfire Night is an exciting time for many, but unfortunately accidents from fireworks are not uncommon. No treatment, or the wrong treatment, can lead to lifelong damage and scarring. If you have taken a first aid course specialising in burns, you can volunteer at your local fireworks display. You'll be able to enjoy the fireworks in the knowledge that, should anything go wrong, you'll be there to help.

December

If you don't want to spend Christmas Day watching repeats on the television, then charities in the homeless sector could do with your support. This doesn't just mean serving up food: Crisis needs all sorts of helpers, from hairdressers to doctors. Alternatively, Age Concern runs schemes over the festive period that include befriending or providing help at home for older people.

7. Volunteering overseas

Volunteering is one of the best ways to truly get to know a new culture and country. And going abroad is not just the preserve of the young. People of all ages and with different experiences have something to offer organisations that work on a diverse range of projects, from training teachers in rural Africa to monitoring wildlife in Central America.

Later in the book we talk about what you need to consider before taking up a voluntary post, but going overseas requires a lot more thought. Before you set your heart on a specific project, it is worth thinking about the following:

How much time can you give?

There are hundreds of overseas volunteering opportunities, lasting from two weeks to two years. Think carefully about how much time you can and want to give. Do you want to use your annual two-week break from work to do something that will benefit others, rather than just lying on a beach? Will your employer support your endeavours with unpaid leave if you decide you want to take a longer break?

If you're a young person thinking of taking a gap year before you start university or after you've graduated, do you want to fit in a bit of volunteering while working your way around the world, or take part in a year-long project?

Do you have specific skills and experience?

While volunteering overseas can enhance and develop new skills, think about what you can offer an organisation. Some voluntary groups require their volunteers to have certain skills, such as in medicine, teaching or healthcare. Others require good communication, writing and language skills, or simply patience and understanding. Think carefully about whether you really do fit the bill. It may sound obvious, but if you're not fond of spending time with children in the UK, you probably won't like doing it overseas. If you're not passionate about the environment or wildlife, don't volunteer to spend a month monitoring dolphins even if it does involve camping on a beach.

What will conditions be like?

Some people like nothing better than to sleep under canvas, use a pit latrine and cook food over a kerosene gas stove. Others want four walls, running water and a regular supply of electricity. It is vital that you think about the conditions you will be living in before you go overseas. If you're heading to a developing country, you will need to bear in mind that life might be more basic. Electricity supplies can be erratic, flushing toilets are rare and the chance to take a bath is almost non-existent. If you really want to get involved in a local community overseas you will undoubtedly have to accept some lifestyle changes. Think about what you could live with, or without. Remember that living side by side with the locals - rather than in an air-conditioned building in the local town - could help you form bonds that will last much longer than the trip.

What about medical help?

Health issues are a consideration. Find out if you will need to take specific medication while you're abroad, such as anti-malaria tablets, or have inoculation jabs before you go. If you have an existing medical condition, speak to your doctor before applying for a project and find out about the health risks involved in working overseas. Ask the voluntary organisation what sort of medical support is available locally and how you can obtain medicine for existing conditions. You will also need to check that any medical problems you have before you go do not affect your insurance cover. Think also about how you will cope with extended periods of heat and humidity. If you head into the shade as soon as the sun comes out in the UK, stay away from hot countries.

Does the organisation have a religious affiliation?

Some organisations do have religious beliefs that underpin their work. While you may not need to be religious yourself, you should feel comfortable with these beliefs. Most religious organisations will be quite upfront about their work and the sort of things they would expect from volunteers. Some religious organisations don't allow volunteers to drink alcohol in certain situations or to form exclusive relationships if working in a team.

What about local customs?

It is important to be aware of the customs and culture of the country or community in which you will be working overseas. The organisation that is sending you abroad should fill you in, but it is always a good idea to do your own research to avoid a social faux pas. For women this is particularly important. In some cultures women are expected to cover their knees and shoulders, or even their whole bodies. Failure to do so could result in unwanted attention. Remember that not all countries will abide by the same social customs as you may be used to, so you may find you are not given the same respect or opportunities as your male counterparts. You may be able to fight these attitudes to a certain extent, but you may have to learn to live with them too.

When should you apply?

Applications for overseas work can take time to process, so it is best to start early. If you're planning to undertake a long-term project, it will be worth beginning your research at least a year before you plan to go.

What support will you get?

Once you've decided on the country you want to visit and what you want to do when you get there, it is important to find out what an organisation is offering in terms of support. Will it pay your travel costs, accommodation and food? Will it pay pocket money while you're out there? Some organisations pay a small wage to long-term volunteers. You may be asked to raise funds to meet the costs of the trip. With some organisations charging anything between £1,000 and £5,000 for an overseas experience, you will need to consider how much time it will take to raise the money.

Find out what back-up you will receive when you get overseas, particularly if there is a medical emergency. Does the organisation have a local office that will help you to settle in and acclimatise to your new surroundings and offer ongoing support? Find out if you will receive any cross-cultural training or language teaching before you leave the UK.

And finally

Once you're out in the field, try to remember the following:

- The first couple of weeks may be hard as you get used to your new surroundings, but remember the excitement you felt when you got accepted on to your project and the reason why you wanted to volunteer overseas in the first place.
- Learn to love the differences – try not to judge things as being better or worse, but instead appreciate the way things are done.
- Volunteering is a two-way thing. You can learn as much from the locals as they can from you.
- Minimise your impact on the environment and use resources thoughtfully, they may not be as abundant as they are at home.
- Buy local products where possible to support the economy of the area. And always pay a fair price when bargaining.
- Think how you can make your volunteering sustainable. Can you train a local person so the work you do can continue after you've gone?
- Make the most of your time overseas. Embrace opportunities, get to know local people and enjoy yourself.

PAT CLARK, 58, from Perth, is a former headteacher. For two years she worked for an NGO in Kampong Cham, Cambodia, through VSO.

I was a headteacher and I decided that I didn't want to just give up, but I wanted to put something back into a society where education could make a real difference. Education helped me out of deprivation and I thought there could be a way I could help. I could give my skills. The appeal of VSO is its focus on what you can give as a person.

I flew out to Cambodia on my 56th birthday and was out there for two years

attached to a local NGO that focused on education, in particular helping girls, which appealed because I was head of a girls' school. We did all sorts of work with the girls, we offered scholarships to stay on at school – the dropout rate among girls is terrible – and helped to develop their skills base. I was involved in curriculum development work, writing materials that were then translated into Khmer.

The biggest difficulty is language. I got a basic grounding, but that was not going to get me to the level at which I could operate in English.

I had a Khmer counterpart, a lovely girl who was 32, and part of my job was to build up her skills, so she learned a lot about styles of work. Things rub off. I think you make a difference just by going there and giving up a bit of your life.

I was based in a town about two hours outside Phnom Penh. It was nice not being in the capital as you get to know people. My exercise on Sunday was cycling round the town and people would always greet you.

It is not so hard going out there, what is hell is coming back. I've been back for eight months and I'm still not adjusted. When you're out there you have to submerge yourself in a new culture, different language and climate and when you come back you just find it really hard. I'm not the only one who has found things hard. It is the materialism. You spend two years among people who didn't have two pennies to rub together, but you were surrounded by love and graciousness. It is a real eye-opener coming back here.

Now I'm back, I intend to do some volunteering work of some sort, maybe something with refugees, but using the skills I've built up.

My advice to anyone thinking of going out with VSO would be to make sure you have your support network in place. Being out there can be very lonely. You need people who are going to email and write letters, the telephone system is dire. My friends sustained me. You make friends out there, but friends back home really help.

I don't want to go back to the tropics, it is quite an assault on your health. But I keep in touch with people I met and I've made some really good friends through VSO. There will always be a bit of my heart labelled Cambodia.

8. Volunteering and the law

While most legal obligations lie with the organisation for which you are volunteering, it is important that you understand the legal and organisational issues that come with getting involved in the voluntary sector.

It is important to understand that as a volunteer, you are not afforded the same legal protection as paid employees, In its book *Volunteers and the Law*, the organisation Volunteering England states that some volunteers who believed they had been treated unfairly were able to argue successfully that their status within an organisation was that of an employee, which means they should be subject to the same treatment as a paid worker. For example, if an organisation imposes a certain number of hours on a volunteer in return for receiving training, and those hours are not completed, the volunteer may be asked to pay the cost of the training. The volunteer could then argue that they were being treated like a paid worker.

The same could be true if an organisation pays regular expenses, even when the volunteer is off sick or on holiday, rather than actual expenses.

Whether a worker is defined as a volunteer or a paid employee will be dependent on whether a contract exists between the organisation and the volunteer, and whether the organisation has charitable status.

Contracts

For the purposes of law, a contract doesn't have to be written down and signed, or be a verbal agreement. A contract is a description of a relationship that exists between an organisation and a volunteer.

Even if neither party has intended that a contract should be created, the relationship between them could be viewed as contractual. If, for example, you, as a volunteer, receive more than your actual expenses (perhaps you automatically get paid travel expenses even though you are in walking distance of the project), or if the organisation has a certain degree of control over the work you are doing and there is an obligation to carry it out, this would be viewed as a contractual relationship.

If the relationship is judged to be contractual by a tribunal, then the volunteer could be regarded as a worker in the eyes of the law, which could, in effect, mean they are entitled to a minimum wage (volunteers are exempt from this) and subject to anti-discrimination laws and paid holiday entitlement.

Apart from actual expenses, the only other benefits you receive as a volunteer should be in training to improve your skills and, if relevant, accommodation or pocket money.

For more information, visit www.volunteering.org.uk.

Equal opportunities

All organisations are obliged by law not to discriminate against workers because of gender, marital status, disability, colour, race, nationality or ethnic origin. This means they have to comply with the current legislation on equal pay, sex discrimination, race relations and disability discrimination. Of course, this legal requirement relates to paid workers, so as a volunteer you will not automatically have the same rights. However, all good organisations will have an equal opportunities policy in place, which they should apply to both paid and voluntary workers. It is always a good idea to familiarise yourself with this policy as you may be able to use it as an argument against any mistreatment.

Benefits and taxes

You should still be entitled to receive welfare benefits if you are only receiving out-of-pocket expenses when you volunteer. If you receive any more than this, you could be classed as a paid employee. Anyone receiving jobseeker's allowance must prove they are still actively seeking work and must not receive any more money than out-of-pocket expenses.

For national insurance purposes, you will not be taxed for simply receiving expenses. However, if you receive some form of regular payment, this will be taxed. There can be a fine line between expenses and regular payment, but the organisation for which you volunteer should be able to put you straight. To prevent any confusion, the organisation must be able to demonstrate that you only receive out-of-pocket expenses, and will keep records. This means you will need to keep hold of any receipts and may be required to fill out an expenses form.

Health and safety

Organisations have a duty of care towards volunteers, so steps should be taken to reduce the probability of an injury, perhaps through training, the use of appropriate safety clothing and supervision. Larger organisations - those with five or more employees - must by law have a written health and safety policy, so it will be worth taking a look at it to find out the obligations placed on the organisation and on yourself. Smaller organisations are likely to have something similar in place as a sensible precaution.

An employer should carry out risk assessment exercises, which must be written down if there are five or more employees, and these should mention what could go wrong for volunteers and how they should be protected. These assessments could look at the potential for accidents or injury, physical, emotional or financial abuse, or if as a volunteer you exceed the boundaries of your role. In the event of an accident, you should be covered by the organisation's insurance.

If an organisation takes volunteers under the age of 18, a more specific risk assessment may be carried out to judge whether they, or the people put in their charge, could be at risk. But a few guiding principles, such as not leaving young volunteers unsupervised, should limit any risk.

If you are not told when you begin volunteering, then find out what the procedures are should you, or someone you are caring for or working with, need medical attention. Who is the person in charge of first aid? Or in case of fire, whose responsibility is it to ensure everyone is out of the building?

If you're working at a computer, you will also need to ensure you take regular screen breaks.

Insurance

All organisations that take volunteers should have an insurance policy to cover them, either under employer's liability insurance or public liability insurance. This mainly protects the organisation in the event of volunteers making negligence claims. Check with the organisation before you start, particularly if you are an older volunteer. Despite the great steps taken to encourage older people to volunteer, some insurance companies will not cover people over the age of 65, which may leave voluntary organisations reluctant to take them on.

If you are involved in an employer-supported volunteering scheme you should be covered by your employer's insurance, even if you are volunteering off site and out of hours. The employer has a duty of care to protect workers from harm whether inside or out of the office, and should have appropriate insurance cover.

Copyright

Be aware that under copyright law, the copyright for any work or material produced by an employee belongs to the employer. No specific mention is made to volunteers, but you might need to talk things through with an organisation before you get cracking on any entries for the annual report or for an important publication or resource. It has been known for a volunteer to refuse permission for an organisation to use their work following a disagreement. In this case there probably needs to be some good grace on both sides. Yes, you can withhold your copyright, but the reason you signed up for volunteering was to give something back.

Working with children and vulnerable adults

Organisations working with children, young people or old people will have a higher duty of care towards them, so as a volunteer you are more likely to be asked for references and given specific training before undertaking any voluntary work. You will be required to undergo background checks by the Criminal Records Bureau to find out if you have any criminal offences and could be banned from working with this group (for more details on volunteering with a criminal record, see page 20). If you are considering doing short-term volunteering work of this nature, it is worth bearing in mind that these checks can take a few weeks to complete. Although a CRB check will only be carried out if you have expressly given your permission, no organisation working in this area should allow you to volunteer if you haven't had one. The voluntary organisations should talk you through what is involved. Try to remember that these checks are done for your protection as well.

Under the law, disclosures made for CRB checks should not be kept for more than six months.

Young adult volunteers

The legal restrictions on employing young people do not apply when it comes to volunteering. As long as the young person's parent or guardian fully understands the nature of the voluntary work, and the hours involved, there should not be a problem.

Volunteer drivers

If part of your volunteering work is to transport people around in your own vehicle, you will need to inform your insurers that you will be using it for voluntary work. Make sure you specifically say you are using your vehicle for voluntary and not commercial work, and that you will only be receiving expenses. In theory this should not increase your premium, but if it does it may be worth shopping around for a better offer. The organisation you volunteer for should reimburse you for any extra expenses that being a voluntary driver brings.

Raising money

There are quite a few legal issues related to raising money for charity. Here are the most important ones:

- You can only raise money for a registered charity.
- All the money you raise must go straight to the registered charity.
- The charity's registered number must be on all fundraising materials.
- To collect money on the street you must be over 16 and sealed buckets must be used.
- All fundraising must be supervised by someone over 18.
- All monies collected must be managed by someone over 18.
- If you hire an external venue for your event check that they have all the correct licenses. A reputable venue will be able to show you the license, their public liability insurance policy and the health and safety policy.

It is also useful to talk to the relevant local authority if you want to organise an outdoor event as applications need to be made three months in advance, but each local authority will work slightly differently. Find out your local council contact at www.upmystreet.com.

Sponsorship and Donations

All requests for donations to charity must have an attached registered charity number. All funds raised by you for the charity must only be received by this charity organisation. Any personal information collected about donors or supporters must only be used only in compliance with the Data Protection Act 1998. When a proportion of the money raised is being used to cover all or some costs, then this must be made clear to donors.

Collections

There are various licenses you might need if you are going to make a collection. For all collections made in public places (areas that the public have unrestricted access to all the time), you must have a Street Collection Licence, which can be obtained from the relevant local authority. These are limited and need applying for a month in advance. If you plan to collect money in a place that is privately owned such as a shopping centre, you will need to get permission from the owner or manager. For business premises, such as pubs, you also need the permission of the owner or manager. A House to House Collection Licence is required for collections that move from place to place and can be obtained from your local authority.

During all collections, you must wear ID badges and use sealed collection tins. All collectors must be over 16.

Raffles and Lotteries

If you want to hold a raffle at a one-off event, you must sell tickets solely at the event. If you do not spend over £250 on prizes (donated prizes do not count) and do not give money prizes (vouchers do not count) it will count as a Small Lottery, for which you do not need a licence. The result of the raffle must also be drawn at the event. If your lottery or raffle does not fit into this description then you will need a Lotteries Licence from your local council or metropolitan borough. Liability for the legal organisation of a lottery falls onto the person/persons promoting it.

The law overseas

Many of the legal issues surrounding volunteering abroad will vary from organisation to organisation. The only concrete advice - and it is probably the most important - is that you will be subject to the laws of the country in which you choose to work. So, while you may have support from a charity or NGO and will probably have access to a British embassy or consulate, if you break the law you will be liable to pay the consequences as that country sees fit. It is important to remember this, as some people who go overseas on behalf of a UK-based organisation think it will bail them out if they get into trouble. While an organisation will offer advice, it is unlikely to be able to overturn the law.

In terms of whether you will be insured while you're abroad, again, this varies between organisations and on the type of work you do. It is vital that you check before you leave exactly what, if anything, you will be covered for by the organisation sending you. Insurance is notoriously difficult to arrange when you're already out of the UK.

Some organisations, such as VSO, will pay national insurance premiums on your behalf while you're overseas, but you will need to check before you go.

DIRECTORY

in association with do-it.org.uk

The Directory has been created in association with do-it org.uk Every effort has been made to ensure the accuracy of the information at the time of going to press. However, many sources are being constantly updated, so if you want to volunteer for one of the organisations in the book, do check their website for the most current information.

ADVOCACY

Advocacy & Information Foundation

Website: www.aif-advocacy.org.uk
Email: info@aif-advocacy.org.uk
Tel: 01642 327583 ext 324 or 01642 835149

Advocacy & Information Foundation works with adults in Teesside who have a learning or physical disability, and with older people and carers, aiming to help them to lead more independent lives.

The Foundation provides free, independent and confidential support and advocacy. It may help people on a one-to-one basis, or in a group setting where people with similar difficulties and experiences work together.

Volunteering opportunities vary widely. Volunteers can:

- act as citizen advocates, working with individuals to help them make decisions and access information and services
- work in publicity, or in office support.

Training is available for those volunteering as citizen advocates. Other training may be available, if needed.

Advocacy Partners

Website: www.advocacypartners.org
Email: info@advocacypartners.org
Tel: 020 8330 6644

Advocacy Partners works with people in London and Surrey who have learning or physical disabilities or mental health needs, and with older people.

The first independent advocacy group in the UK, it aims to help individuals with disabilities or who are older to have more choice and independence, exercise their rights, participate in society and become less isolated.

Advocacy Partners offers advice and information, helps an individual to identify concerns, represents a person's views if necessary and offers group support. Advocates can also help people to make key life decisions and to develop their confidence. The group works with approximately 1,000 people each year.

Volunteers can:

- work with individuals, one-to-one, helping them with issues such as resolving problems with social services, health and housing
- work in roles that use their own professional skills, such as information technology or human resources
- become members of the group's board of trustees.

BATIAS Independent Advocacy Service

Website:www.batias.com

Email: batias@btopenworld.com orbatiasinfo@yahoo.co.uk

Tel: 01375 389869

BATIAS, a registered charity, provides advocacy for adults with learning disabilities in Essex.

The organisation aims to help people with learning disabilities to make decisions, gain access to information or services, and participate in the community. It also offers help with self-advocacy, on a one-to-one basis or in groups. Advocates work out of three offices, in Southend, Grays and Brentwood.

Volunteers can work as citizen advocates, working with one individual. No special training is required, although volunteers are always matched with a person with similar interests. Other volunteering opportunities include promoting the charity's services at community events, or helping with transport and fundraising.

Volunteers are trained in health and safety, first aid and communication, and about barriers that those with a learning disability may face. All volunteers receive supervision and support.

ANIMALS

Bat Conservation Trust

Website: www.bats.org.uk
Email: enquiries@bats.org.uk
Tel: 020 7627 2629

The Bat Conservation Trust (BCT) works to protect and conserve the UK's bats. With around 4,000 members, the BCT carries out much of the practical work involved in monitoring bat populations and their habitats across the country. The BCT works on the conservation of bats for everyone, from keen bat watchers such as colony counters and roost visitors, to casual bat fans who are happy to sit back and read Bat News.

Bat groups across the UK provide a network of volunteers, rescuing and caring for sick, injured or downed bats, and rehabilitating them for release back into the wild. Bat groups also provide many of the voluntary bat wardens who provide free advice and information to people who find bats in their houses.

Most regional groups have members involved with projects such as the BCT's National Bat Monitoring Programme. The BCT runs a number of national annual surveys through a volunteer network to monitor the status of many bat species across a range of habitats. These surveys form the National Bat Monitoring Programme, through which changes in bat populations are tracked.

Regional groups also carry out their own fieldwork, including bat box surveys and inspections of underground sites, looking for hibernating bats. Many groups organise training programmes for people who wish to become licensed bat workers. They also run a wide range of events, walks and talks.

Blue Cross

Website: www.bluecross.org.uk
Email: info@bluecross.org.uk
Tel: 01993 822651

The Blue Cross is a registered UK animal welfare charity which aims to ensure the welfare of animals by providing practical care and promoting a sense of respect and responsibility towards animals in the community. It provides support to the nation's pets and their owners by treating pets whose owners cannot afford private veterinary treatment, finding permanent homes for unwanted animals and providing education on responsible animal ownership.

Its team of specially trained staff care for up to 85 horses and ponies at any one time, and monitor 350 more that have been loaned to homes across the country. The Blue Cross also has a fleet of animal ambulances to transport animals owned by housebound people to and from the London veterinary hospitals, a series of mobile clinics, and out-of-hours emergency services at the Victoria and Grimsby hospitals.

Its adoption centres, equine centres and hospitals each have their own volunteer coordinator, and the work of Blue Cross volunteers depends on the skills and preferences of the individual. It has a growing nationwide network of trained volunteers who speak to classes of children in primary schools and to youth groups. The education team works closely with schools and provides education resources, including a curriculum-linked programme for primary schools.

In addition to this, the Pet Bereavement Support Service (PBSS) is dedicated to offering support and understanding to bereaved pet owners through a national network of trained volunteer telephone and email befrienders.

British Union for the Abolition of Vivisection

Website: www.buav.org
Email: volunteer@buav.org
Tel: 020 7700 4888

The British Union for the Abolition of Vivisection (BUAV) is an anti-vivisection campaigning organisation that works for lasting change by challenging attitudes and actions towards animals worldwide.

The BUAV is dedicated to defending the rights of animals and the wellbeing of people by raising awareness, exposing animal experimentation and creating meaningful changes in policy. Through public campaigning, undercover investigations, media activities, political lobbying, promotion of cruelty-free products, legal and scientific expertise and educational and information materials, the BUAV aims to spread its campaign message to as wide and diverse an audience as possible.

The BUAV is at the centre of international campaigns to end animal experiments. As a founder and key member of the European Coalition to End Animal Experiments (ECEAE), the BUAV works with animal rights groups across Europe to coordinate campaigning initiatives and ensure that laboratory animals are high on the European political agenda.

Volunteers can support the BUAV during office hours to help with anything from assistance with campaign events to data entry (training is provided on Raiser's Edge and Excel). There are also volunteering opportunities for those who have specialist skills such as IT or science backgrounds.

Care for the Wild International

Website: www.careforthewild.org
Email: info@careforthewild.com
Tel: 01306 627 900

Care for the Wild International (CWI) is an animal welfare and conservation charity helping animals – from snow leopards to badgers – to fight for survival. It funds practical projects around the world to make areas safe from poachers, rehabilitate sick or injured animals and provide sanctuary for those that can't return to the wild. It also works to expose animal cruelty and wildlife crime through research, education and advocacy. CWI aims to get quick and efficient emergency aid - food, veterinary equipment, medicines and housing - to the animals that need it most.

CWI works with local people to shape attitudes towards wildlife conservation in those communities closest to wildlife reserves. In Britain it aids rescue centres and animal protection groups throughout the country, helping a variety of wildlife, such as foxes, otters, seabirds, seals and dolphins. Overseas, it supports work in Africa, Asia and elsewhere, to protect endangered animals such as tigers, elephants, gorillas, turtles and rhino.

The CWI also uses scientific expertise to support campaigns for wild animal protection at key forums such as the Convention on International Trade in Endangered Species and commissions important animal welfare and ecological investigations.

The organisation uses volunteers who work alongside paid staff handling promotional material, publicity, mail order, fundraising activities and appeals. In addition to administrative volunteers, volunteer fundraisers raise important funds for the CWI's work, mainly by holding sponsored events.

Cats Protection

Website: www.cats.org.uk
Email: helpline@cats.org.uk
Tel: 08702 099 099

Through a nationwide network of 29 adoption centres and 261 voluntary-run branches, Cats Protection (CP) re-homes around 60,000 cats and kittens every year.

With increasing demands placed upon CP by a growing domestic and feral feline population, over 6,000 volunteers carry out the majority of the charity's work. Volunteers look after many of the 7,000 cats and kittens that can be in the charity's care at any one time. Cats for re-homing are cared for by fosterers in their own homes. In addition to the cat re-homing work, CP volunteers carry out many important tasks to run their local branch, such as bookkeeping, home visiting, driving and transportation, public relations and fundraising.

CP branches, run entirely by volunteers, span the length and breadth of the country, from Uist in the Outer Hebrides to Helston in Cornwall.

Branch volunteers often have day jobs and work voluntarily for CP in the evenings and at weekends.

Compassion in World Farming

Website: www.ciwf.org.uk
Tel: 01483 521950

The mission of Compassion in World Farming (CIWF) is to advance the wellbeing of farm animals worldwide. The organisation believes that cruelty and suffering is an unnecessary product of modern farming and aims to end it by way of consumer education, public awareness programmes and welfare campaigning.

Its vision is the promotion of compassionate, respectful treatment of farm animals and the end of cruel factory farming practices.

Through peaceful lobbying of governments, food standard agencies and food retailers, international media collaboration and undercover investigation, CIWF is committed to exposing and reducing poor farm animal welfare standards associated with factory farming systems and long-distance transportation of farm animals. CIWF seeks to achieve the global abolition of factory farming worldwide and advocates organic, humane and sustainable alternatives. It supports those systems that improve the living standards of farmed animals.

Volunteers can participate in the CIWF's work through:

- fundraising
- street collections
- helping out at community stalls and events

Horses and Ponies Protection Association

Website: www.happa.org.uk
Email: enquiries@happa.org.uk
Tel: 01282 455992

The Horses and Ponies Protection Association (HAPPA) is a charity for equine welfare. An example of the type of work it carries out is fighting against the transportation of large horses to the continent for slaughter.

Its welfare officers have wide-ranging expertise on all aspects of equine welfare and are conversant with the law concerning cruelty to animals. They investigate over 800 cases of cruelty and neglect each year, offering advice and support where possible and preventing cruelty by intervention and prosecution where necessary.

HAPPA has been instrumental in achieving better protection for horses with the Riding Establishments Act, the Ponies Act 1969, the Illegal Tethering Act 1991 and by setting up the National Equine Welfare Committee 1997. It continues to campaign for improvements to existing legislation to ensure that horses, ponies and donkeys are protected from cruelty and neglect.

HAPPA has two fully equipped rescue centres that work to bring rescued and abandoned animals back to health. It never sells these horses, ponies and donkeys. Instead, all suitable animals are placed in private homes through HAPPA's legally

binding loan scheme. Those with special needs continue to be cared for at the most appropriate HAPPA rescue centre.
HAPPA uses a range of volunteers in many roles, such as:

- events organiser
- events team member
- collecting box coordinator
- administrator
- helper at its visitor centre

Mammal Society

Website: www.abdn.ac.uk/mammal
Email: enquiries@mammal.org.uk
Tel: 020 7350 2200

The Mammal Society works to protect British mammals, halt the decline of threatened species, and advise on all issues affecting British mammals.

The Mammal Society's main aims are:

- to involve people of all ages in its efforts to protect mammals and promote mammal studies in the UK and overseas
- to raise awareness of mammals, their ecology and their conservation needs
- to educate people about British mammals by providing current information on mammals through its publications
- to monitor mammal population changes and survey British mammals and their habitats in order to identify the threats they face
- to broaden people's understanding of British mammals

Volunteers can join their local mammal group and take part in local mammal recording and surveying as well as participating in a wide range of talks and events.

Mayhew Animal Home

Website: www.mayhewanimalhome.org
Email: info@mayhewanimalhome.org
Tel: 020 8969 0178

The Mayhew Animal Home offers a variety of community services, providing advice, care and assistance to animals and their carers. The Mayhew provides shelter and care for cats, dogs, rabbits and a variety of other animals, and the organisation believes that animals have a value beyond economic measure and that they are entitled to legal, moral and ethical consideration.

Volunteers can get involved in two different ways:

- For those who do not have much time to spare on a regular basis, there are general roles, including kennel, cattery and rabbit volunteers, home visitors, cat and dog fosterers, drivers and event stallholders.

- Those who can commit to a specific number of hours each week may apply for specific roles in a more formal way, including an interview for the role. Examples of these roles include cat trappers, receptionists, adoption officer assistants, animal groomers, theatre porters, laundry and general cleaning helpers, daily drivers for dog runs, fundraising office assistant, education officers, Kids Club leaders and photographers.

Monkey Sanctuary Trust

Website: www.monkeysanctuary.org
Email: info@monkeysanctuary.org
Tel: 01503 262532

The Monkey Sanctuary Trust is an environmental charity dedicated to promoting the welfare, conservation and survival of primates, particularly woolly monkeys.

It works to end the primate trade and abuse of primates in captivity. Other work of the Trust includes promoting the rehabilitation of primates to natural habitats and conserving natural habitats through education and sustainable living.

The Trust is based at the Monkey Sanctuary in Cornwall, home to a colony of woolly monkeys and a small group of rescued ex-pet capuchin monkeys. The aim is to provide a stable setting in which the monkeys, rescued from lives of isolation in zoos or as pets, can live as naturally as possible. The Trust provides advice and support for primate rescue centres around the world.

Keepers care for the monkeys and are assisted by volunteers who are involved in the day-to-day running of the sanctuary. Although volunteers cannot help directly with handling animals, they do assist the organisation by:

- Preparing food for the monkeys
- Running the shop
- Serving in the kiosk
- Running workshops in the activity room
- Helping to keep the sanctuary tidy
- Helping at the admission desk
- Answering visitors' questions at the enclosures

In the winter, volunteers help to maintain and clean the house and monkey territory, design and make displays and work in the sanctuary gardens. Volunteers with special practical skills have helped to build new enclosures and improve the monkey territory.

Organisation Cetacea

Website: www.orcaweb.org.uk
Email: volunteer@orcaweb.org.uk
Tel: 0845 108 6454

Organisation Cetacea (ORCA) provides information on and works to protect cetaceans – whales, dolphins, seabirds and other marine wildlife. It conducts offshore surveys in European waters, with a major focus on the Bay of Biscay and the English Channel. By joining ORCA, members are encouraged to learn more about whales and dolphins and to go out and see them, thus raising awareness of the problems that cetacea face.

One of ORCA's objectives is to provide politicians with information that will give them the incentive to prioritise improved conservation measures. ORCA is working in partnership with other research and conservation organisations, providing up-to-date information on the distribution and relative abundance of cetaceans and the threats that they face. Data collected by ORCA volunteers is published in an annual report, which is distributed to 3,000 people in over 20 countries worldwide. In addition, ORCA's information is used by a range of researchers and conservationists to aid their own research and campaigns.

The organisation has developed a network of volunteers trained to collect information. Their network of surveyors includes volunteer observers travelling on board ferries, cruise ships, cargo vessels and yachts, as well as dedicated research vessels. These observers have contributed 3,500 cetacean sightings involving over 35,000 animals in more than 45,000 kilometres of European waters.

Volunteers can help with a wide range of tasks, from data collection in the field to promoting the rich diversity of the marine environment, and can also help to raise support funds for ORCA.

People's Dispensary for Sick Animals

Website: www.pdsa.org.uk
Email: volunteers@pdsa.org.uk
Tel: 0800 854 194

Leading veterinary charity the People's Dispensary for Sick Animals (PDSA) exists to provide free veterinary treatment to the sick and injured pets of people in need, and promotes responsible pet ownership.

There are many different volunteer roles available, from sorting stock or creating window displays in one of PDSA's 181 shops, to office-based administration roles and participating in local fundraising groups.

PDSA treats more than 4,650 sick and injured pets every working day at its 47 UK-wide PetAid hospitals. There are a limited number of volunteer roles available within PetAid hospitals, such as kennel assistants and receptionists, but these do get snapped up quickly.

PDSA also relies on its volunteers to raise much-needed funds to continue its vital work for pets in need of vets.

Royal Society for the Prevention of Cruelty to Animals

Website: www.rspca.org.uk
Email: volbacs@rspca.org.uk
Tel: 0870 33 35 999

The Royal Society for the Prevention of Cruelty to Animals (RSPCA) works to prevent cruelty and promote kindness to animals, and to alleviate their suffering. The RSPCA aims to achieve its mission through education and campaigning and also by running animal centres, wildlife centres and hospitals.

The RSPCA is a charity that receives no lottery or state aid and its running costs are funded exclusively by voluntary contributions. Most volunteering activities for the RSPCA do not involve practical animal care, although there are some opportunities to get involved in dog walking or cat socialising. RSPCA branches undertake a wide range of work in their local area, which is reflected by the variety of roles carried out by volunteers, including:

- Welfare work
- Fundraising
- Shop work
- Trusteeship

Volunteers with the RSPCA have many different skills, but any training that may be needed for the role is provided.

Royal Society for the Protection of Birds

Website: www.rspb.org.uk
Email: volunteers@rspb.org.uk
Tel: 01767 680 551

The Royal Society for the Protection of Birds (RSPB) exists to conserve wild birds and to secure a healthy environment for birds and other wildlife.

The RSPB's work includes:

- Campaigning
- Protecting, restoring and managing habitats for birds and other wildlife
- Researching problems facing birds and the environment
- Carrying out recovery projects for many threatened species

The RSPB also helps to tackle international conservation issues through BirdLife International, a global partnership of conservation organisations.

The RSPB was founded by volunteers and they continue to support the charity in many important ways. Work can be indoors or out, at home or on a reserve. Volunteers bring a range of skills, from computing to project management and from administrative support to language interpretation.

Whale and Dolphin Conservation Society

Website: www.wdcs.org
Email: info@wdcs.org
Tel: 0870 870 0027

The Whale and Dolphin Conservation Society (WDCS) is a charity dedicated to the conservation and welfare of all whales, dolphins and porpoises through conservation, research and education projects.

WDCS has a national network of volunteer public speakers who give educational talks about whales and dolphins, the threats they face and how WDCS is involved in helping to protect these animals. Aided by a 'speaker pack' which includes notes and slides, speakers give talks to a range of interested groups from schools to scouts, from wildlife groups to the Women's Institute.

Volunteers also distribute leaflets. WDCS's 'Adopt a Dolphin' and 'Membership and Anti-captivity' campaign leaflets are aimed at recruiting new supporters and informing the public about the work of WDCS.

There are also opportunities to get closer to whales and dolphins. WDCS works closely with the Tethys Institute, which offers places for paying volunteers to join two of their cetacean research projects in the Mediterranean and Greece. Funds raised from the holidays go directly to supporting research work.

ARTS AND LEISURE

Action Factory

Website: www.actionfactory.org
Tel: 01254 679335

Action Factory is an arts company that works to build confident, unified communities through encouraging participation in cultural and creative activity.

It works towards improving access to the arts and creating new audiences by developing, managing and delivering participatory workshops and projects in various art forms.

Volunteering with Action Factory involves working with a variety of people in a variety of communities. It delivers workshops and projects in a range of settings, including schools and colleges, youth and community groups, festivals and events, voluntary and campaign groups, health agencies and housing and regeneration initiatives.

Consequently, volunteers with Action Factory contribute a variety of skills and experiences. Wherever possible, volunteering opportunities are tailored to match individuals' needs and expertise.

Apples & Snakes

Website: www.applesandsnakes.org
Email: info@applesandsnakes.org
Tel: 020 7924 3410

Apples & Snakes curates, hosts and acts as a partner to facilitate and promote performance poetry through live events across the UK. It was established as a platform for poetry that would be popular, relevant, cross-cultural and accessible to the widest range of people.

It arranges special events, tours and festivals throughout the year to promote new poets and joint productions with other poetry organisations. It also stages live shows in schools, prisons and young offender institutions to develop literacy and communication skills, motivation and self-esteem.

Apples & Snakes acts as a resource base offering advice, information and recommendations on various aspects of poetry for new and established poets, promoters, television, radio and publishers.

There are opportunities for volunteers in education, programming and press and marketing. Activities range from helping to set up before a poetry performance to full project management. Examples of the kind of work volunteers have undertaken in the past include writing and editing updates for the website, running poetry workshops and researching authors for an anthology. The type of work that is carried out by any volunteer is decided by the projects that Apples & Snakes is working on and how much time a volunteer can commit.

Volunteers receive an induction covering issues related to equipment and health and safety and an introduction to staff members.

Volunteers can have free entry to Apples & Snakes shows for the duration of their time working with the company.

The Art Fund

Website: www.artfund.org
Tel: 020 7225 4863

The Art Fund works to help UK museums collect works of art.

Falling public funding and rising market prices have put the ability of UK museums to collect art under threat. With the support of their members, the organisation has offered more than 600 museums and galleries around the UK over 850,000 works of art.

In addition to this, the Art Fund does other work to support UK museums. It offers around £4 million in grants annually to museums and galleries around the UK. It also led the campaign to extend free admission to all national museums and galleries, which achieved success in 2001.

Volunteers bring many different skills to the Art Fund. They organise and promote events, raise awareness through giving talks, write articles for the local press, distribute leaflets and raise funds. Training is provided where necessary.

The Art House

Website: www.the-arthouse.org.uk
Email: info@the-arthouse.org.uk
Tel: 01924 377740

The Art House, established in response to access problems faced by disabled artists, works to provide everybody with equal access to facilities and opportunities in the visual arts and crafts.

The organisation provides opportunities for artists by creating exhibitions, projects and commissions. It enables artists to develop their creative practice and vocational skills by providing advice, information, training and experience. It also enables artists to share skills and exchange ideas by creating networking opportunities between artists.

The Art House also produces the Good Gallery Guide, a web-based guide to art galleries across the UK.

In 2008, the Art House building in Wakefield will be opened. This building will have studios for both long-term and short-term rent, together with short-term accommodation for visiting artists. A community studio will ensure that the building is used by the wider community. This project aims to provide access and support to disabled artists that will enable them to work alongside their non-disabled colleagues.

Volunteers maintain the website, write features, visit galleries and provide feedback. Further opportunities for volunteers in the Art House building in Wakefield will include supporting artists in the community studio and disabled artists in their studios, as well as providing general support for visiting artists and artists in residence.

Chickenshed

Website: www.chickenshed.org.uk

Tel: 020 8351 6161

Chickenshed is an inclusive theatre company that is open to everybody. It was founded on a belief in the value of the creativity in everyone and anyone.

Work produced ranges from full-scale productions with casts of 250-plus and a 20-strong band, through intimate studio pieces spotlighting solo performers, to original works devised by the company through workshops. The company also presents adaptations of classic plays and stories and pioneering dance, with unique movement and melodies and lyrics composed by Chickenshed underpinning it all.

Chickenshed welcomes volunteers to work at the theatre, in front-of-house roles, in the office, backstage or in the bar.

Create to Learn

Website: www.createtolearn.com

Email: info@createtolearn.com

Tel: 020 7785 6392

Create to Learn is an initiative that encourages schoolchildren to discover a love of the arts. University arts students work with school pupils to develop creative projects, ranging from papier-mâché sculptures to short animations. At the end of the academic year there is a public exhibition or performance that showcases the pupils' work.

Create to Learn provides an opportunity for undergraduate and postgraduate students to develop their project management and delivery skills and to establish links with galleries and theatres. It also offers volunteers the chance to be mentored by creative arts professionals, who can share their knowledge of working in the industry.

Volunteers attend a two-day training session, which covers issues such as child protection, planning and delivery of projects and evaluation. That is followed by a 20-hour placement delivering the project in the school. This is spread over the course of an academic year and includes at least one session shadowing a teacher. Throughout the year, they are given the opportunity to attend at least four sessions with a creative mentor. Volunteers work towards achieving the Community Arts Leader Award at the end of the year, which recognises their ability to deliver successful creative projects for children.

Creative Corners: the Global Arts Project

Website: www.creative-corners.com
Email: enquiries@creative-corners.com
Tel: 0845 466 7091

Creative Corners is a not-for-profit agency specialising in creative volunteer projects. A registered community interest company, they donate all profits to associated charity Arts for Change to set up music and arts centres in the orphanages and homes for disadvantaged, abused and abandoned children where their projects are based.

Staff members work individually with volunteers to plan projects to use their skills in creative ways. Creative Corners recruits teachers, performing artists, creative enthusiasts, gap year students, career breakers and grown-up gappers to use and develop their skills running volunteer projects across South and Central America. Volunteers pay a project fee, which includes insurance and accommodation, to take part in projects ranging from two weeks to over a year.

Projects are diverse, with past and present schemes including:

- Play devising in a Bolivian orphanage
- Teaching photography to street kids in Honduras
- Singing with teen mothers in Nicaragua
- Teaching jewellery and design skills to orphaned boys
- Work in a Brazilian social circus
- Redecorating a children's home in Guatemala
- Designing a garden in a Peruvian orphanage

Eastside Educational Trust

Website: www.eastside.org.uk
Email: online@eastside.org.uk
Tel: 020 7033 2380

Eastside Educational Trust promotes independent learning through the use of the creative arts and is committed to raising young people's language and literacy standards.

It runs workshops, after-school clubs, holiday projects and in-school training days for teachers. The Trust prioritises work with children and young people in London but also runs national and international projects.

Eastside's workshop facilitators are experienced arts practitioners who use their professional skills to motivate and inspire the next generation of writers, artists and performers. They include writers, poets, comedians, actors, performers, singers, dancers, musicians, composers, directors, choreographers, visual artists and filmmakers.

Eastside has a resource centre that features a library of arts and education resources, a training space and a workshop space.

Volunteers help to run workshops and events, contribute to reports and briefings, and assist with day-to-day office administration. There are also opportunities to help out in the resource centre library.

English PEN

Website: www.englishpen.org
Email: enquiries@englishpen.org
Tel: 020 7713 0023

English PEN is a writers' association providing an active and supportive focus for people working in the literary sector. It exists to promote literature, protect writers' freedoms and provide a platform for the free exchange of ideas.

PEN runs a diverse events programme for both members and the public which aims to pull together the different strands of their work.

PEN has three main programmes:

- Readers and Writers attempts to widen literary culture by arranging author visits to children and adults in disadvantaged communities.
- Writers in Prison supports writers throughout the world whose human rights are threatened.
- Writers in Translation awards funds to support new books being published for the first time in English translation.

Volunteer activities include editing and updating the website, contributing to the members' newsletter, helping to recruit new members and setting up visits by authors to schools and prisons. They can also help PEN by writing letters to writers, publishers and potential sponsors; assisting with the running of talks with authors and film-makers; and drafting appeals on behalf of oppressed writers.

Fine Cell Work

Website: www.finecellwork.co.uk
Email: enquiries@finecellwork.co.uk
Tel: 020 7931 9998

Fine Cell Work is a charity that teaches needlework to prison inmates and sells their embroidery and soft furnishings to the general public. Tapestry, quilting, embroidery and appliqué skills are taught to the highest level, as Fine Cell Work aims to show that prison work can be amongst the best quality on offer. Styles range from traditional to contemporary and personal pieces are commissioned.

Prisoners often send their earnings to their children and families, use them to pay debts or put them towards accommodation upon release.

The teaching is all done by volunteers, many of whom are members of the Embroiderers Guild and the Royal School of Needlework. All volunteers are given training by Fine Cell Work.

Other opportunities to support the charity include sorting and preparing embroidery materials and assisting at sales events nationwide.

Hatton Street League

Website: www.streetleague.co.uk
Email: info@streetleague.co.uk
Tel: 020 8536 5330

Hatton Street League is a charity that uses sport to help young adults from disadvantaged backgrounds – many of whom are homeless – to achieve their potential.

It works to engage individuals through a range of sporting projects that aim to build confidence and self-esteem, promote inclusion through team ethos, develop transferable skills, provide support towards employment and encourage participants to live healthy lifestyles.

Hatton Street League runs football and fitness projects in London and Glasgow. It is a member of the Streetfootballworld network, an organisation connecting football projects tackling social issues around the world.

During match days and cup competitions, volunteers can assist with player registration, pitch-side management, manning refreshment stations, photography, surveys and interviews, match reports and management of equipment and kit. There is also the opportunity to volunteer as a referee.

Alternatively, volunteers can assist coaches at training sessions and become volunteer team managers or mentors. They could also choose to help with fundraising events or administration.

Finally, there are opportunities for volunteers to help out at its offices, with work ranging from new team research, marketing, press and PR to IT support and accounts.

Making Music

Website: www.makingmusic.org.uk
Email: info@makingmusic.org.uk
Tel: 0870 903 3780

Making Music, the National Federation of Music Societies, is a not-for-profit membership organisation representing and supporting amateur and semi-professional music groups of all genres throughout the UK. It has approximately 2,400 groups in membership – from brass bands to samba groups, handbell ringers to orchestras, music clubs to barbershop choruses.

It provides a range of artistic and administrative services and training opportunities for its members, both performers and promoters.

Making Music also lobbies national and local government and other agencies on behalf of voluntary music making.

Opportunities for volunteers include:

- Applying for funding
- Commissioning new music
- Taking part in national initiatives such as the Listen Up! National Festival of Orchestras series or the Adopt-a-composer scheme
- National and regional training programmes to help groups with their marketing, fundraising and project development
- Running the music exchange scheme, allowing members to borrow music from one another for the cost of a handling fee
- Providing ad hoc support in the office including updating the website, research and marketing
- Helping to run award schemes for young musicians
- Organising local events

The October Gallery

Website: www.theoctobergallery.co.uk
Email: web@octobergallery.co.uk
Tel: 020 7242 7367

The October Gallery is an art gallery dedicated to the appreciation of art from cultures around the world. It exhibits the work of 'transvangarde' artists, such as William Burroughs, who incorporate elements from other cultures into their work.

As well as exhibitions by individual artists, the Gallery shows cutting-edge contemporary art produced in one culturally continuous region. The Gallery also hosts theatre, dance and concert performances and evenings with writers, poets and thinkers.

The October Gallery's education department aims to communicate some of the stylistic diversity of contemporary art from around the world through workshops and outreach projects.

It works with schools and community groups on artist-led outreach programmes. These projects, including art workshops with victims of torture and storytelling workshops for elderly people, emphasise collaborative work rooted in the art exhibited at the Gallery.

Volunteers should contact the Gallery for information on how they can participate.

SportsAid

Website: www.sportsaid.org.uk
Email: mail@sportsaid.org.uk
Tel: 020 7273 1975

SportsAid helps young sports people start out in their chosen sport, giving them independent recognition and financial help.

At the 2004 Athens Olympics, Britain had 17 gold medallists. SportsAid had supported 15 of them.

SportsAid works closely with each National Governing Body (NGB); these bodies nominate young athletes to SportsAid for help.

SportsAid is also at the heart of the Talented Athlete Scholarship Scheme (TASS). This is a government-backed programme which supports young sporting talent, and is specially designed to cater for the special needs of athletes within the education system. The programme aims to reduce the number of talented athletes who drop out of sport due to academic and financial pressures. It works through the provision of a tailored package of services, comprising coaching, sports medicine, sport science, etc. It aims to ensure that young athletes have the optimal level of support to train and compete whilst studying.

Volunteers can help by:

- Forming a corporate partnership
- Fundraising by running the London Marathon
- Assisting at one of SportsAid's events
- Helping in their regions by providing local knowledge as governors

Women's Radio Group

Website: www.womeninradio.org.uk
Email: wrg@zelo.demon.co.uk
Tel: 020 8995 5442

Women's Radio Group (WRG) works in partnership with media training organisations and community groups in the UK and abroad to develop women's opportunities in radio.

WRG works on various projects, for example:

- Working with Desi Radio to provide training in radio production for people from the Punjabi community, and with London Link Radio
- Running courses covering a range of subjects including short basic radio production courses, drama writing and production, digital editing, presentation skills and voiceover techniques
- Arranging networking seminars and events on themes such as how to pitch programme ideas and using radio to support projects in developing countries

Volunteers are involved in both producing and presenting radio programmes. Where necessary, training is given on how to operate digital equipment, build programmes and present shows.

CAMPAIGNING AND INTERNATIONAL DEVELOPMENT

Action Against Hunger

Website: www.aahuk.org
Email: info@aahuk.org
Tel: 020 8293 6190

Action Against Hunger, a non-governmental organisation, works to combat hunger and malnutrition worldwide.

The organisation aims to ensure that people have access to food during and after situations such as war, conflict, natural disaster and when people face longer-term distress. It operates mostly in the developing world.

During emergencies, it provides food and water. Its longer-term programmes focus on rehabilitation and sustainable development, with the ultimate goal of fostering autonomy and self-sufficiency. The organisation provides training in areas such as nutrition, food security, healthcare, and water and sanitation.

Volunteers can help to:

- organise events and fundraisers
- provide personal contacts and administrative support
- assist with public outreach, PR and campaign work

Action for Children in Conflict

Website: www.actionchildren.org
Email: info@actionchildren.org
Tel: 01793 767 820

Action for Children in Conflict is a charity working with young victims of conflict.

The charity aims to help children and young people by providing psychological, emotional and educational support that will help in the short-term and make future conflict less likely.

It funds projects in Kenya and northern Uganda and has previously worked in Sierra Leone, Tanzania, the UK and elsewhere.

Its services include facilities at which survivors receive support. If young adults want to start their own business, the charity may provide business training and start-up micro-credit.

It also supports street children, working with communities and families to prevent children leaving home and on rehabilitation for those already on the streets. Rehabilitation might include education and skills training.

Volunteers need have no special skills, although some have a background in social work, child care, management, administration, fundraising or publicity. Volunteers can also work in the charity's five shops in Oxfordshire.

Action for Southern Africa

Website: www.actsa.org
Email: actsa@actsa.org
Tel: 020 7833 3133

Action for Southern Africa, a non-governmental organisation, works to help the people of southern Africa.

It aims to foster peace, democracy and development in the region. It does this through lobbying, campaigns, publication of reports and informing the media. It also collaborates closely with other groups, especially trade unions.

Action for Southern Africa campaigns on a number of issues, including:

- the practices of mining companies and other businesses operating in the region
- fair trade
- access to Aids drugs and treatments
- rebuilding Angola after the country's 27 years of civil war

Volunteers can work with the organisation's local groups in the UK, helping with fundraising events and publicity. At the organisation's main UK office in London, volunteers can help with both campaigning and fundraising.

Afghanaid

Website: www.afghanaid.org.uk
Email: info@afghanaid.org.uk
Tel: 0871 288 1144

Afghanaid, a non-governmental organisation, works with rural communities in Afghanistan.

It aims to help the communities to find long-term sustainable solutions to everyday problems and to involve local people in its projects.

The organisation works with more than 500,000 adults and children.

Afghanaid's projects include:

- vocational training for women
- improving agriculture with a view to eliminating food shortages
- building roads, bridges and dams
- teaching the basics of sanitation to improve standards of health
- training local people involved in its programmes in subjects such as conflict resolution and the concerns of children

Volunteers can work for the organisation in the UK, but not overseas. Opportunities include office work, collecting donations, running photographic exhibitions, fundraising or operating stalls at various events such as music festivals.

Amnesty International

Website: www.amnesty.org.uk
Email: activism@amnesty.org.uk
Tel: 020 7033 1500

Amnesty International, a non-governmental organisation, works to protect internationally accepted human rights.

Through research and campaigning, it aims to ensure that all people enjoy the human rights described in the Universal Declaration of Human Rights adopted by the United Nations in 1948.

Amnesty operates a wide variety of campaigns, including those that seek to:

- abolish the death penalty, torture and other forms of cruel and degrading treatment or punishment
- protect refugees, asylum seekers and non-combatants in armed conflicts
- ensure fair trials for political prisoners
- secure the release of all prisoners of conscience
- end violence against women
- implement arms control

Volunteers can work in the organisation's offices in London, Edinburgh, Belfast and Cardiff. They must commit to a minimum of three months of volunteering. Roles might include helping with:

- campaigning
- marketing
- media relations
- administrative support

Anti-Slavery International

Website: www.antislavery.org
Email: info@antislavery.org
Tel: 020 7501 8920

Anti-Slavery International, founded in 1839, works to eliminate slavery and related abuses. It is a non-governmental organisation which lobbies governments of countries where slavery still exists to eliminate the practice. It supports research to assess the scale of slavery, and it works to raise awareness about the issues of slavery and human trafficking. The organisation has projects at local, national and international levels.

Anti-Slavery International has been involved in various endeavours, including:

- the campaign to improve conditions for rubber workers in the former Belgian Congo
- the campaign to stop child slavery in Hong Kong
- the effort to combat slavery in Niger, Nepal, and west Africa

Volunteers can work in the organisation's offices. A time commitment of three months is usually required.

Azafady

Website: www.azafady.org
Email: mark@azafady.org
Tel: 020 8960 6629

Azafady is a charity that runs development and conservation projects in south-east Madagascar.

The charity's projects focus on:

- health and sanitation
- sustainable livelihoods
- conservation
- infrastructure development
- research
- reforestation
- community education.

Primarily it aims to help the Antanosy people in southeast Madagascar to protect the local environment, including some of the last remaining stands of indigenous coastal forest.

There are three volunteering options with Azafady: Pioneer Madagascar, Lemur Venture and London-based office work.

- Pioneer Madagascar offers the opportunity to take part in a range of practical construction work, conservation research and educational activities alongside village communities with an international team of experienced project leaders.
- Madagascar is the planet's native home of lemurs and Azafady's Lemur Venture is a volunteering initiative set up in collaboration with PBZT, Madagascar's national botanical and zoological gardens, to help to protect the species. Volunteers work on initiatives focused on the study and maintenance of lemur populations, including gathering information as part of international captive breeding programmes.
- In its London office Azafady is always keen to find willing and able helpers for a multitude of tasks, from photocopying to marketing and project administration.

Bees for Development

Website: www.beesfordevelopment.org
Email: info@beesfordevelopment.org
Tel: 01600 713648

Bees for Development is a non-governmental organisation that works to support poor beekeepers in developing countries. The organisation aims to alleviate poverty and help people to build a sustainable future through beekeeping.

Its activities include:

- compiling and distributing technical and training information
- putting people in touch with each other to share information and skills

- undertaking research
- advocating policy changes that could benefit poor beekeepers

The organisation publishes a variety of materials and maintains an online information centre. Its work is supported by a charitable trust which raises funds for the projects.

Volunteers can work in the organisation's office near Monmouth, helping to administer projects and publications. Volunteers who have specialist skills and knowledge that could directly help beekeepers in developing countries may advertise in the Bees for Development journal.

Book Aid International

Website: www.bookaid.org
Email: info@bookaid.org
Tel: 020 7733 3577

Book Aid International, a non-governmental organisation, provides books for poor people in sub-Saharan Africa and Palestine.

It mainly provides books for rural and urban libraries that loan books without charge and are accessible to everyone. It also aims to help its partner libraries in sub-Saharan Africa and Palestine to strengthen their role in the local community.

In addition, the organisation supports the growth of publishing and bookselling in sub-Saharan Africa and Palestine so that more books can be published that are affordable and that reflect the local languages and culture.

Book Aid International works in 18 countries in sub-Saharan Africa and in Palestine, providing over half a million books and journals each year to libraries, hospitals, refugee camps and schools.

Volunteers can work in the following areas:

- at the organisation's library and warehouse in Camberwell in south London, where help is needed to sort, shelve, stamp and pack books.
- at the main office in Camberwell, assisting with the programmes, fundraising, communications or resources.
- collecting books from donors around the UK and arranging for them to be delivered to the office.

The organisation does not send volunteers overseas.

The Catholic Agency for Overseas Development

Website: www.cafod.org.uk
Email: cafod@cafod.org.uk
Tel: 020 7733 7900

The Catholic Agency for Overseas Development (CAFOD) works to combat poverty, mostly in the developing world, on behalf of the Catholic church in England and Wales.

The Agency aims to promote long-term development, respond to emergencies, raise public awareness, promote social justice, and speak out on behalf of poor communities.

It works with partner organisations on projects including those designed to:

- ensure reliable food supplies
- help with reconstruction after disasters and economic development
- increase awareness about Aids and HIV

The agency also campaigns to raise awareness about issues such as debt in the developing world and fair trade.

Volunteers can work in the agency's regional offices, with local parishes or in schools to help children and young people to understand issues related to overseas development and relief. They can also help with publicity.

Some opportunities are available in the agency's head office in Brixton, south London. The time commitment is usually for one or two days weekly, for a minimum of three months.

The agency does not send volunteers overseas. Volunteers do not have to be practising Catholics, but some knowledge and understanding of the church is required.

Challenges Worldwide

www.challengesworldwide.com
info@challengesworldwide.com
0845 2000 342

Challenges Worldwide, a charity, is the largest agency in Scotland that matches professional volunteers with assignments overseas.

It aims to match volunteers from the UK with three to six-month assignments, mostly in developing countries. The charity works with a core set of partner organisations in India, Sri Lanka, Bangladesh, Belize, Ghana, Croatia and Bosnia. These partner organisations deliver services or run projects in the following areas:

- health
- education
- environment and conservation
- human rights
- poverty alleviation

Volunteers are matched according to their professional skills and experience, which may be in communications, business development, human resources or law.

Volunteers work on defined projects that are designed to help partner organisations to become more self-sufficient and productive over the longer term. Challenges Worldwide works with the partners over a period of two to five years, or more if required.

ChildAid to Russia and the Republics

Website: www.childaidrr.org.uk
Email: info@childaidrr.org.uk
Tel: 020 8460 6046

ChildAid to Russia and the Republics is a charity working with disadvantaged children and young people in Russia, Ukraine, Moldova and Belarus.

The charity tries to improve the quality of life for street children, orphans and children with disabilities by working with local partners to deliver short and long-term aid and development.

The charity:

- supports projects that provide hot meals, shelter and vocational skills
- works in orphanages and implements schemes to encourage foster parenting
- provides education, quality residential care and family support for children with disabilities

Volunteers with childcare or paediatric experience or qualifications can work with the charity's partners in Russia, Ukraine, Moldova and Belarus. Volunteers without special skills can work in the charity's summer or winter camps.

Childhealth Advocacy International

Website: www.caiuk.org
Email: office@caiuk.org
Tel: 01782 712599

Childhealth Advocacy International works with children and pregnant women in countries where there is extreme poverty, armed conflict or other disaster.

Based in Newcastle-under-Lyme, the organisation currently aims to improve the health treatment offered to women and children in Albania, Bosnia, Cameroon, Burma, Pakistan, Sri Lanka, Uganda and Zambia, and is planning projects in Gambia.

Activities include:

- designing and offering training in emergency treatment appropriate for hospitals and clinics with few resources
- running outreach services which take hospital clinics out into the community
- helping to equip paediatric wards
- running projects for children and pregnant women that treat a variety of life-threatening health problems

Volunteers can help with computing, graphic design or marketing, by creating and distributing publicity materials, or by running fundraising activities.

Christian Aid

Website: www.pressureworks.org.uk
Email: volunteering@christian-aid.org

Christian Aid, a charity, works to combat poverty and injustice in some of the world's poorest countries.

Set up in 1945 by churches in Britain and Ireland, it supports local organisations in the developing world and also operates through its own 16 offices overseas. It helps people regardless of their beliefs or religion.

Its projects range from building a community well or a village school to responding to crises, such as in the Middle East and Sudan. The charity also campaigns to change policies and highlight worldwide issues such as awareness of HIV and Aids, trade, climate change and corporate accountability.

Volunteers can help with:

- fundraising
- campaigning
- organising events
- collecting money during the charity's fundraising week
- assisting in the charity's head offices in London

Concern

Website: www.concern.net
Email: londoninfo@concern.net
Tel: 020 7738 1033

Concern, a charity based in Dublin, works with the poorest people in developing countries.

It works directly with the poor, and with local and international partners, on issues such as education, fair trade, health, Aids prevention and treatment and by responding to emergencies. Its projects are worldwide, including in Haiti, Niger, Sierra Leone, the Democratic Republic of Congo, Sudan, Ethiopia, Eritrea, Tanzania and Rwanda. The campaigning arm of Concern raises public awareness.

Although based in southern Ireland, the charity has offices in Belfast, London and Glasgow and an affiliated organisation in New York.

Volunteers can work in:

- fundraising
- research
- helping with the food aid programme, a fundraising campaign for schools that supports the charity's work overseas
- administration

The Fairtrade Foundation

Website: www.fairtrade.org.uk
Email: mail@fairtrade.org.uk
Tel: 020 7405 5942

The Fairtrade Foundation, one of 20 similar groups internationally, aims to ensure that marginalised farmers and other producers, mostly in Africa, Asia and Latin America, are getting a fair deal.

It also oversees licensing of fair trade products in the UK. The licence is to ensure that producers receive a minimum price, including enough to cover the cost of sustainable production and to invest in community development.

The Foundation monitors labour, health and environmental conditions in the workplace, and works to introduce new fair trade products and to update the certification standards for existing products. It attempts to raise awareness about fair trade through leaflets, posters and the media.

In March each year, it holds Fairtrade Fortnight, when groups across the country link up with supermarkets, health food shops, churches and schools to promote fair trade.

Volunteers can work in any one of five departments:

- commercial relations
- communications
- certification
- finance
- resources

Volunteers can also work on specific events, or help to convert a local café, school or college to using fair trade products.

Global Disaster Relief Fund

Website: www.gdrf.org.uk
Email: info@gdrf.org.uk
Tel: 020 7629 8456

The Global Disaster Relief Fund is a charity that raises and provides money for disaster relief.

The fund aims to give immediate cash assistance to provide food, shelter and funding for those who have the greatest need, in order to minimise further suffering. In extreme situations, the fund can launch an emergency appeal to help those affected quickly.

Volunteers are deployed in teams, after a disaster, to help to collect donations and organise specific fundraising events. Volunteers can also carry out street collections. Fundraising is carried out across the UK.

Global Vision International

Website: www.gvi.co.uk
Email: info@gvi.co.uk
Tel: 0870 608 8898

Global Vision International (GVI) provides volunteers, promotion and direct funding to numerous conservation and humanitarian projects in more than 30 countries.

GVI works with local partners to promote sustainable development through environmental research, conservation, community development and education. Partners range from international charities and not-for-profit groups to governmental organisations.

Volunteer projects include:

- marine conservation in Africa, Mexico and the Seychelles
- community projects in Latin America and Asia
- conservation expeditions in Patagonia and the Amazon

GVI's international partners and beneficiaries include the Dian Fossey Gorilla Fund (International), Rainforest Concern, the Jane Goodall Institute, the Endangered Wildlife Trust and the South African National Parks.

No previous experience is necessary as full training is given.

Goal

Website: www.goal-uk.org
Email: info@goal-uk.org
Tel: 020 7631 3196

Goal, a charity based in Dublin, works with poor people in the developing world.

It aims to ensure that people have access to food, water, shelter, medical attention and primary education both ongoing and during crises such as armed conflict and the Aids and HIV epidemic.

The charity offers practical assistance and has responded to many major natural and man-made disasters over the past 29 years. Over the longer-term, Goal offers rehabilitation programmes, such as ensuring that there is primary healthcare available, and repairing homes and infrastructure.

It also helps to provide new clinics, schools, water and sanitation facilities, and prioritises programmes for street children and people affected by Aids. It works on social and economic development, and it advocates and campaigns on issues such as corruption, international arms trading and child trafficking.

Volunteers, known as Goalies, can work on the charity's programmes in the developing world. There are also opportunities to volunteer at the head office in Dublin.

Handicap International

Website: www.handicap-international.org.uk
Email: hi-uk@hi-uk.org
Tel: 0870 774 3737

Handicap International, a charity, provides long-term support and emergency relief for disabled people in countries affected by poverty and conflict.

Handicap International is active in about 60 countries. Some of its activities are:

- supporting rehabilitation and preventing accidents causing disability, for example from treading on unexploded mines. Its rehabilitation services are provided directly to local organisations.
- arranging post-emergency relief, including providing artificial limb fitting and rehabilitation following the earthquake in Pakistan in 2005.
- as part of its strategy of prevention, raising awareness of the disabling effects of illnesses such as HIV/Aids.
- lobbying for the inclusion of the disabled in all aspects of daily life, including employment.

Volunteers can work with the charity on a regular basis in the office, or during one-off events.

HealthProm

Website: www.healthprom.org
Email: healthprom@healthprom.org
Tel: 020 7284 1620

HealthProm, a small non-governmental organisation, works with communities in eastern Europe and central Asia to bolster the health and social care of women, infants and children.

Its projects aim to ensure the availability and accessibility of information and services for local healthcare providers and for mothers and children. Its schemes provide training and guidance on topics ranging from safe childbirth, newborn care and infection control to child mental health and care for children with disabilities.

Volunteers can work in office-based roles including:

- research
- writing
- fundraising
- promotion
- administration

Most volunteers work for a minimum of three months, but shorter-term assignments may be available.

The organisation is also developing a network of events committees staffed by volunteers to raise funds and promote awareness in their local community. The

London office supports such groups, putting them in touch with potential volunteers, and providing training, materials and assistance.

Volunteers who are health and social care professionals can work on the content and delivery of projects. Three years' teaching experience is required. Such work usually involves up to three weeks' input a year and may involve work in the project country.

Health Unlimited

Website: www.healthunlimited.org
Email: e.michau@healthunlimited.org
Tel: 020 7840 3777

Health Unlimited is a charity that works to provide healthcare to communities in the developing world.

It works with local people to provide services designed to address long-term health needs, rather than emergency relief. Health Unlimited aims to help people to develop skills as health workers, to organise their community, and to improve their health.

The charity also offers advocacy, especially for indigenous peoples who may face discrimination, exclusion or persecution. It works in 15 countries across Africa, Asia and Latin America; 95% of its staff are local people.

Volunteers can help with office-based work in the UK, including:

- fundraising
- publicity
- organising events
- research and administration
- helping with the charity's programme team in London

Students in international development can sometimes volunteer within the programme team.

Indicorps

Website: www.indicorps.org
Email: info@indicorps.org
Tel: 07973 401 522

Indicorps, a non-governmental organisation, encourages Indians around the world to participate in development work in India.

Its work is based on a fellowship programme designed to encourage leadership and civic participation among Indians in local projects in India that address social or economic issues. Projects have included:

- eco-clubs for children
- micro-credit for women
- Aids awareness among adolescents

Volunteers become fellows, each of whom makes a year-long commitment. They are expected to live on a basic stipend, using public transport and other local services.

Indicorps assists potential volunteers in finding suitable placements through its Indiserve platform. Indicorps is also developing a volunteer programme for management-level experts and retiring professionals.

i-to-i

Website: www.i-to-i.com
Email: uk@i-to-icom
Tel: 0870 333 2332

i-to-i is a provider of ethical volunteer travel and TEFL (Teaching English as a Foreign Language) training.

Every year i-to-i sends 5,000 people to work with over 500 projects in community development, teaching, sports coaching, media and conservation. It is involved in 28 countries across Africa, Asia, Australasia, Central America and South America.

Projects include:

- working with street children in Rio de Janeiro
- building homes in Kenya
- conservation work in Honduras
- community work in southern India

The organisation, through its charity arm, the i-to-i foundation, also provides funding for projects. It raised money for the rehabilitation of Sri Lanka after the tsunami of 2005, paying for tools and equipment.

i-to-i projects in general are open to anyone aged 18 or over, with a handful accepting over-16's. Projects range from one to 24 weeks. i-to-i also offers a number of tours, providing the opportunity to combine worthwhile work with travel. Employee volunteering programmes are also available, enabling companies to send their staff to work on the projects.

Medact

Website: www.medact.org
Email: info@medact.org
Tel: 020 7324 4739

Medact, a charity, works on health issues such as those linked to the war in Iraq, the lack of healthcare in Africa and climate change.

It undertakes education, research and advocacy on the health implications of conflict, economic and social change, and environmental issues. Most of its work relates to the developing world. Its members are healthcare professionals.

Medact was formed by a merger of two organisations: the Medical Association for the Prevention of War, founded during the Korean war as a medical lobby for peace, and the Medical Campaign Against Nuclear Weapons.

Volunteers usually work on defined tasks involving administrative support, research, or writing for the webpage. Most volunteers work at the head office in London.

Merlin

Website: www.merlin.org.uk
Tel: 020 7014 1600

Merlin, a UK charity, works to provide healthcare and medical relief for people who face natural disaster, conflict, disease or a collapse of their health system.

The charity aims to deliver basic healthcare during a crisis and to help to build services that provide long-term healthcare. It works with local organisations and communities in countries as diverse as Afghanistan, Burma, Georgia and Kenya. Volunteer opportunities are available in the UK, in the London office, and overseas as part of Merlin's internship programme.

Mines Advisory Group

Website: www.magclearsmines.org
Email: maguk@mag.org.uk
Tel: 0161 236 4311

Mines Advisory Group (MAG), a non-governmental organisation, works in some of the world's poorest countries clearing and destroying abandoned weapons, unexploded munitions and landmines.

By clearing weapons, it improves people's access to education, healthcare and trade, to water and to land for cultivation.

MAG's projects include those intended to:

- open up access routes between villages
- help the construction or reconstruction of housing, schools, health centres and other infrastructure
- boost the local economy by employing staff from the affected communities
- destroy illegal stockpiles of munitions, small arms and light weapons

The group works in Angola, Cambodia, Democratic Republic of Congo, Iraq, Laos, Lebanon, Sri Lanka, Sudan and Vietnam. It has worked in a total of 35 countries. MAG is a co-laureate of the 1997 Nobel Peace Prize, awarded for its work with the International Campaign to Ban Landmines.

Volunteers can donate time in the UK, helping with fundraising events and activities by selling T-shirts, collecting cash and handing out leaflets. The events often take place during evenings or at weekends.

Minority Rights Group International

Website: www.minorityrights.org
Email: minority.rights@mrgmail.org
Tel: 020 7422 4200

Minority Rights Group International, a non-governmental organisation, works with ethnic, religious and linguistic minorities and indigenous groups worldwide.

The organisation seeks to secure the rights of minority and indigenous people and to educate the general public about the issues they face. Founded more than 30 years ago, it has 130 partners in 60 countries.

It publishes training manuals, briefing papers and workshop reports and offers training on international minority rights and advocacy techniques. It lobbies and works with international bodies such as the United Nations and the European Union to campaign for minority and indigenous groups and to promote international human rights.

Volunteers must work for a minimum of eight weeks full time, or three months part time. They can help with general administration, such as logistics, filing, photocopying, preparing correspondence, and collating information and training materials.

There may be opportunities to help with organising events and fundraising. Volunteers can also work on specific projects that require a working knowledge of a particular language, specialist knowledge or experience.

No More Landmines Trust

Website: www.landmines.org.uk
Tel: 020 7471 5580

The No More Landmines Trust, a charity, raises awareness about landmines and raises funds to clear them and rehabilitate survivors.

The campaign aims to educate people about the problems that landmines can cause. Landmines kill and injure civilians and deny people access to farmland and water long after wars are over, despite the widespread banning of their use.

Apart from the clearance of unexploded landmines and weapons, the charity funds rehabilitation, including physical, economic and psychological help for disabled people. It is the UK partner in the global Adopt-A-Minefield campaign, which also has partners in the US, Canada and Sweden.

Its funds are mostly used for charitable purposes, but it also gives grants for non-charitable purposes when appropriate. The charity has funded the clearance of minefields in six countries: Afghanistan, Bosnia-Herzegovina, Cambodia, Croatia, Mozambique and Vietnam.

Volunteers can help in the charity's office, or work for the charity from home or during events. The trust keeps a database of volunteers with particular professional skills who are called on if needed, such as:

- law
- computing
- finance
- PR and marketing
- graphic design
- auctioneering

In addition, volunteers can run their own fundraising events and undertake sponsored activities to raise money for the trust.

Ockenden International

Website: www.ockenden.org.uk
Tel: 01483 772012

Ockenden International is a charity that works with refugees and with people displaced by conflict or natural disaster.

The charity aims to help people to rebuild their lives after man-made or natural disaster. It works with the communities themselves, and with local institutions or organisations.

Ockenden runs projects in Afghanistan, Cambodia, Iraq, Nepal, Pakistan and Sudan dealing with topics such as Aids, poverty, conflict and education. The charity offers help to the communities for as long as it is needed.

Volunteers can participate in sponsored fundraising events.

One World Trust

Website: www.oneworldtrust.org
Email: info@oneworldtrust.org
Tel: 020 7766 3470

One World Trust promotes education and research into global organisations, ranging from major businesses to not-for-profit or inter-governmental groups.

It aims to help to eradicate poverty, injustice and war by making such global organisations more responsive and accountable. A charity, it focuses its work on three international issues:

- accountability
- sustainable development
- peace and security

The charity works with other organisations on a number of its projects, and is a special consultant to the economic and social council of the United Nations. It also educates political leaders and opinion-makers on the findings of its research.

The groups it studies have ranged from the IMF to Toyota, Nestlé and Amnesty International.

Volunteers can become interns, usually for three or six months. They work on topics such as peace and security, parliamentary oversight of foreign policy and organisational accountability.

Specific tasks might include:

- researching, writing and editorial support
- general administrative support
- helping to organise events
- maintaining databases and networks

Internships often require a degree in a subject related to international relations, global development or international law.

Oxfam Great Britain

Website: www.oxfam.org.uk
Tel: 0870 333 2700

Oxfam Great Britain is an advocacy and relief agency working globally on poverty and suffering.

A charity affiliated with Oxfam International, it aims to help eradicate poverty and suffering through:

- aid
- support and protection during emergencies
- longer-term programmes and projects
- campaigning

It works on issues such as trade, education, international debt and aid, health, Aids, gender equality, conflict and natural disaster, democracy and human rights, and climate change. The charity operates with international governments and global institutions, local communities and individuals.

Volunteering opportunities vary widely. Volunteers can assist in the charity's shops, or work at the head office in Oxford or in any of seven regional offices. Tasks might include organising events, sending supporters information, website design, human resources, fundraising and auditing the network of shops. Oxfam does not send volunteers overseas.

People & Planet

Website: www.peopleandplanet.org
Email: people@peopleandplanet.org
Tel: 01865 245678

People & Planet is a student network that campaigns on the issues of international poverty, human rights and the environment.

Founded in 1969 as Third World First, it works to encourage students to become involved in tackling social and environmental issues. Its main campaigns are in trade and the developing world, climate change and Aids.

The campaigns include strategies to:

- raise awareness about fair trade and encourage British schools, colleges and universities to use fair trade products
- raise awareness about climate change and renewable energy
- lobby the UK government to prioritise Aids, and increase access to treatment and drugs in the developing world

Volunteers can help with organising and running events, including stewarding at large events, and run sponsored events of their own.

Philippine Indigenous Peoples Links

Website: www.piplinks.org
Email: info@piplinks.org
Tel: 020 7095 1555

Philippine Indigenous Peoples Links, or PIPLinks, is a small organisation that supports indigenous and rural people in the Philippines and elsewhere.

Also known as Indigenous Peoples Links, the network aims to promote the rights of indigenous and other land-based people to maintain and develop their culture, live according to their beliefs, and to control and benefit from their land and resources.

It provides information and educational support to indigenous organisations, advocates on their behalf, and provides links to wider groups. Its focus is primarily on the Philippines. Issues it works on include the development of mining, dams and logging, and people who have been displaced because of conservation projects or conflict. The network is mainly funded by the charities CAFOD, Christian Aid and Trócaire.

Volunteers can help with managing resources and research or by becoming a member of the organisation's voluntary board, which is made up of experts and partners based both in the UK and the Philippines.

RedR-IHE

Website: www.redr.org
Email: info@redr.org
Tel: 020 7233 3116

RedR-IHE, an international non-governmental organisation, provides recruitment, training and support services for humanitarian professionals around the world.

It aims to relieve poverty, sickness and suffering by providing a database of experienced people who want to work on projects that address humanitarian crises. It has programmes in Sri Lanka, Sudan, Kenya and Pakistan.

The charity provides training and support for relief workers. Courses might cover topics such as environmental health during emergencies, and management of people and projects. The courses can count towards formal schemes of continuing professional development.

Volunteers work in office-based roles, usually in London, providing administrative support to departments such as external relations, recruitment or corporate services.

Reprieve

Website: www.reprieve.org.uk
Email: info@reprieve.org.uk
Tel: 020 7353 4640

Reprieve, a charity, works and campaigns to defend people facing the death penalty and other human rights violations.

The charity works through investigation, legal representation, campaigning and education, especially on cases and issues that could have a wider impact.

It prioritises the cases of: the innocent; people who are mentally ill or learning disabled; women, racial and ethnic minorities; all those on death row following what it believes is a miscarriage of justice; and those detained in controversial circumstances during the 'war on terror', for example in Guantanamo Bay, Cuba.

Reprieve also defends those on death row who cannot afford a lawyer. Its work may include legal representation, investigation in the field, forensic testing, finding expert witnesses, and seeking government support in the cases of British nationals.

Its outreach programme aims to provoke debate about the death penalty and related human rights violations. It produces publications, conferences, a website and public events including theatre.

There are two main opportunities for volunteering:

- Volunteers who oppose the death penalty can work in the field on capital cases. Reprieve's advocacy programme trains human rights workers to operate in the field as volunteers or as fellows. These volunteers and fellows work on projects or take up positions in the US or Caribbean for anything from three months to two years.
- There are also opportunities for volunteering in the UK, most often in Reprieve's head office in London. The work might include reviewing and managing case files, legal or internet research, organising events and outreach activities, helping to produce Reprieve's magazine or general administrative tasks. Volunteers may be able to do research from home.

Results

Website: www.results-uk.org
Email: info@results-uk.org
Tel: 01926 435 430

Results, a grass-roots non-governmental organisation, works to end hunger and poverty.

An international lobbying group, it aims to create the public and political will to eliminate hunger and the worst aspects of poverty through lobbying politicians and changing public opinion.

The organisation has developed training, coaching and programmes of support to help individuals to voice their opinions on anti-poverty measures. It also backs lobbying for more funds to fight diseases such as tuberculosis, and works to maximise the effectiveness of that funding.

It lobbies on financial issues, such as micro-finance or micro-credit for very poor people who want to become self-employed. It also campaigns to make education more widely available.

Volunteers can join a local Results group in the UK, part of a network that is coordinated by a full-time member of staff.

Survival

Website: www.survival-international.org
Email: info@survival-international.org
Tel: 020 7687 8700

Survival, an international organisation, works with tribal groups around the world.

The organisation aims to help tribal peoples, especially those most recently in contact with the outside world, to defend their lives, protect their land and determine their own future.

It often works closely with local indigenous organisations, using education, advocacy and campaigning to meet its goals. Registered as a charity in the UK, Survival has supporters in 82 countries and works with hundreds of tribes.

The charity directs its campaigns at all organisations that it believes are violating tribal peoples' rights, from governments, companies and banks to guerrilla armies and missionaries. Its tactics include:

- organising letter-writing campaigns
- holding vigils at embassies
- lobbying decision-makers
- putting forward cases at the United Nations
- drafting international law
- informing tribes of their legal rights
- organising headline-grabbing stunts

Volunteers can work in all departments at the charity's offices, including in press, publications, research and campaigns, outreach, and administration. Volunteers who can donate specific skills, such as computer work or graphic design, may be able to work from outside the offices.

Sustain

Website: www.sustainweb.org
Email: sustain@sustainweb.org
Tel: 020 7837 1228

Sustain, a charity, is an alliance working to improve food and agricultural policies and practices.

It aims to improve the health and welfare of people and animals, protect the environment, enrich society and culture, and promote equity by ensuring that food and agricultural policies are publicly accountable as well as socially and environmentally responsible.

The alliance also seeks to encourage businesses to produce, process and market foods that it believes are good for health and the environment.

It disseminates information, promotes its activities to the media and policymakers, develops networks of members, and advises and negotiates with governments and regulatory bodies. It has produced an extensive range of publications, and represents about 100 non-governmental organisations.

Campaigns have included:

- promoting better food in schools and targeting junk food advertising aimed at children
- encouraging hospitals to use local, organic food
- lobbying to change UK and European policy and international trade rules that relate to agricultural products and food

Volunteering opportunities include administration, research and campaigning.

TackleAfrica

Website: www.tackleafrica.org
Email: info@tackleafrica.org
Tel: 01892 533 100

TackleAfrica is a charity that uses football to raise awareness among young people in Africa about HIV and Aids.

It aims to use the sport to break down barriers to communication, challenging stigma and misconceptions about the disease, helping people to protect themselves, and mobilising communities.

The charity does this through volunteer-led projects such as football tours and coaching, and though community tournaments organised by local partner organisations in Africa.

The charity also advocates, by campaigning in the UK about HIV/Aids in Africa and helping to raise funds for partner organisations.

Volunteers can participate in projects in Africa, or help out with logistics and administration in the UK.

Teaching & Projects Abroad

Website: www.projects-abroad.co.uk
Email: info@projects-abroad.co.uk
Tel: 01903 708300

Teaching & Projects Abroad sends volunteers to 21 developing countries to live and work.

The organisation aims to be the link between the skills and energy of volunteers and the needs of the developing world. Volunteers work in jobs such as teaching, medical work, care, conservation and journalism.

Volunteer placements have included:

- working on human rights law in Ghana
- working on an eco-farm in India
- helping with drama projects in Romania
- teaching children French in Senegal or computer skills in Sri Lanka
- working in a burns unit in Bolivia

Placements can be chosen to suit the interests and skills of volunteers. The minimum age for volunteering is 17 and there is no maximum age.

Volunteers usually live with host families and work with local people. They choose their own dates to start and finish a project, year-round. There is a minimum commitment of one month.

Tibet Foundation

Website: www.tibet-foundation.org
Email: office@tibet-foundation.org
Tel: 020 7930 6001

The Tibet Foundation, a charity, works to create greater awareness of Tibetan culture and the Tibetan people.

The charity runs three main aid programmes:

- The first programme, Aid to Tibet, helps Tibetans living in China, in the territory of Tibet, through education, healthcare and development.
- The second programme, Buddhism in Mongolia, was established to assist Mongolians in their revival of Buddhism. It includes educational and publishing projects that seek to address some of the issues facing Mongolian Buddhism today.
- The third programme, Tibetans in Exile, helps Tibetans living in India and Nepal. The

programme is run in cooperation with the Central Tibetan Administration, the exiled Tibetan government in Dharamsala in India.

To provide long-term care, the trust primarily operates sponsorship schemes. It also organises Tibetan cultural events in the UK and brings a Tibetan doctor to the UK approximately every three months to give talks and perform private consultations.

Volunteers can help with translation, graphic design, research and fundraising.

Tourism Concern

Website: www.tourismconcern.org.uk
Email: info@tourismconcern.org.uk
Tel: 020 7133 3330

Tourism Concern works to reduce the social and environmental problems connected with tourism overseas.

It aims to increase local benefits by working with communities in destination countries and with the tourism industry in the UK. The organisation is based on the belief that tourism often causes or exacerbates poverty and that it does not offer enough benefit for local industries, resources and culture.

The organisation's educational programmes, in schools and universities and in public settings, seek to link tourism to development issues and to promote tourism that helps communities to become more sustainable. Its programmes include talks and lectures, workshops and exhibitions.

Volunteers can work at the London office on campaigns, outreach, research or general office work.

United Nations Volunteers

Website: www.unvolunteers.org

United Nations Volunteers promotes volunteering that contributes to sustainable human development worldwide.

The volunteer arm of the United Nations, it provides opportunities for mid-career professional people to serve as volunteers and contribute to reaching the UN's goals in combating poverty, hunger, disease, illiteracy, environmental degradation, and discrimination against women. The UN has set targets that must be attained by 2015.

The programme aims to foster work at the local level, especially to improve access to basic services, to help disadvantaged people, and to mobilise communities. It also seeks to promote collaboration amongst developing countries.

In just one year, the programme has collaborated with non-governmental organisations, governments and others to deploy about 8,400 volunteers to 140 countries. The volunteers worked on issues such as democratic governance, energy and the environment, crisis prevention and recovery, and Aids.

In South Africa 155 volunteers, many of them from Africa, worked as part of a programme to help to address the loss of skilled people because of the Aids pandemic. They helped national and local public administrations with projects to improve planning mechanisms and policy design, and to create village task forces.

Volunteers can apply online.

Voluntary Service Overseas

Website: www.vso.org.uk
Email: enquiry@vso.org.uk
Tel: 020 8780 7500

Voluntary Service Overseas (VSO) is a charity that recruits professional volunteers to work in international development.

Volunteers live and work in communities in any of 34 countries worldwide. Volunteers usually have a professional qualification in their field, which may range from education or health to business. They must have a minimum of two years' experience.

Working alongside local colleagues, volunteers share their skills and seek to leave their local colleagues with improved knowledge, skills and confidence. The charity has many overseas partners, ranging from governments to community-based organisations, who request volunteers with skills they lack.

Specific professionals requested include those who have worked as doctors, nurses, occupational therapists, managers from the private, public and voluntary sectors, teaching, marketing and advocacy specialists, small business managers, information technology specialists, and mechanical engineers.

For 18 to 25-year-olds with less work experience, the charity offers two programmes:

W Global Xchange is a six-month exchange of teams of 18 young people from the UK and a developing country. The programme is run in collaboration with the British Council, Community Service Volunteers and overseas partners.

W Youth for Development offers a one-year overseas placement for young people who have a year's experience of community or voluntary work. It aims to provide work experience and the chance to promote international understanding and awareness of development issues.

The charity also works with various ethnic minority organisations in the UK to support people who want to volunteer in their countries of heritage.

WaterAid

Website: www.wateraid.org.uk
Email: wateraid@wateraid.org
Tel: 020 7793 4500

WaterAid is an international organisation that works to ensure that people in developing countries have access to clean water, sanitation and education about hygiene.

It aims to help local organisations to plan and set up low-cost, sustainable projects using technology that can be managed by the community itself. WaterAid also seeks to influence the policies of governments and other organisations to try to make sure that access to affordable water and sanitation is protected.

WaterAid operates in 17 of the poorest countries in Africa, Asia and the Pacific region. They are Burkina Faso, Ethiopia, Ghana, Madagascar, Malawi, Mali, Mozambique, Nigeria, Tanzania, Uganda and Zambia in Africa; Bangladesh, India, Nepal and Pakistan in Asia; and Papua New Guinea and Timor-Leste in the Pacific region.

Volunteers can work for WaterAid in the UK, in an office or assisting at an event. Because WaterAid helps local organisations and community groups in the various countries to become active in their projects, volunteer opportunities are not available overseas.

World Wildlife Fund

Website: www.wwf.org.uk
Email:supporterrelations@wwf.org.uk
Tel: 01483 426444

World Wildlife Fund (WWF) is a global conservation organisation that has been instrumental in making the environment a matter of world concern. In addition to funding and managing countless conservation projects throughout the world, WWF continues to lobby governments and policy-makers, conduct research, influence education systems, and work with business and industry to address global threats to the planet by seeking long-term solutions.

WWF-UK works on both global and local environmental issues. Much of its work is in areas where the most critically endangered wildlife and the least-protected habitats are found. However, the origins of many environmental problems lie in developed countries, including the UK – for example, our consumption of natural resources. That is why WWF-UK not only directs some 70% of its conservation expenditure towards its global programmes but also seeks to influence global environmental issues through responsible actions in the UK.

WWF-UK cannot offer direct volunteering opportunities at its offices and projects either in the UK or overseas, but it relies on volunteers to organise events and undertake campaigns. Online campaigners send a letter or e-mail to a decision-maker whenever there's an opportunity to influence environmental policy or legislation or to lobby against environmentally damaging practices. Volunteers are provided with a draft letter (which can be amended) and all the details of who to send the letter to, whether it's a local MP or a government minister.

Volunteers also help out at events to raise money for WWF's work, and they can organise their own events or take part in overseas events such as trekking the Great Wall of China or cycling from Havana to Trinidad.

COMMUNITY

Citizens Advice

Website: www.citizensadvice.org.uk
Tel: 08451 264 264

Citizens Advice, a network of charities, helps people to resolve their legal, money and other problems by providing free information and advice from over 3,000 branches.

Its trained volunteers help people to resolve nearly 5.5 million problems every year. The national charity sets standards for advice and supports bureaux with information, training, publicity and other services, and by lobbying policymakers.

The network uses thousands of volunteers yearly. Volunteers may work as advisers, administrators, receptionists, trustees, campaigners and IT support coordinators. Other opportunities include PR and marketing, fundraising, volunteer recruitment and peer education.

All advisers receive free training, which includes a five-day course run by Citizens Advice. Volunteers are supported throughout the training by a staff member.

Crime Concern

Website: www.crimeconcern.org.uk
Email: info@crimeconcern.org.uk
Tel: 01793 863 500

Crime Concern is a national charity that works with individuals and communities to reduce crime and create safe environments.

The majority of Crime Concern's work is helping young people to stay safe and out of trouble. The charity tries to help young people to get back into education or get a job. It has programmes that aim to reduce anti-social behaviour, and it works with those over the age of 16 who have committed crimes.

Crime Concern also has other projects such as:

- a one-stop community safety service in Kilburn, north London
- restorative justice services in Suffolk
- a programme to help street workers in Southampton to leave prostitution

Volunteers can act as mentors or help to organise and supervise activities. Specific skills are not necessary.

Crimestoppers

Website: www.crimestoppers-uk.org
Tel: contact via website only

Crimestoppers, a charity, works to identify, prevent, solve and reduce crime.

The charity aims to break the wall of silence that often surrounds crime and which can prevent it being solved. Through the charity's free national phoneline, anyone can pass on details of a crime anonymously. If a reward is available, it is paid without compromising the anonymity of the caller. The charity also runs a youth programme designed to help young people to avoid committing crimes.

Volunteers can work as local board members, serving as a link to the community by promoting the charity, in fundraising or in other ways. They work closely with full-time staff.

Liberty

Website: www.liberty-human-rights.org.uk
Tel: 020 7403 3888

Liberty works to promote human rights and civil liberties.

It aims to ensure that all people can exercise their democratic and legal rights. It works on issues such as terrorism, torture, asylum, equality and free speech.

Liberty lobbies the government about laws relating to civil liberties and human rights. It challenges laws by taking test cases to the English and European courts.

It also provides advice to the public, voluntary sector organisations and lawyers through specialist phonelines, letters clinics and its advice website. Because of the way the legal system is organised, much of its work is in England and Wales.

Voluntary positions are advertised on its website.

London 21 Sustainability Network

Website: www.london21.org
Email: office@london21.org
Tel: 020 8968 4601

London 21 Sustainability Network works for a cleaner, greener, more sustainable London.

The group operates a number of projects, including the London Sustainability Weeks, a series of events designed to support people who work on sustainable development in their communities. It also seeks to enable ethnic minority groups to contribute to the welfare of their local environment.

It produces several types of publication, including:

- a directory of projects on sustainability in London
- the London Green Map, which shows community projects
- directories and maps of information and projects for each borough

Volunteers can work in a wide variety of roles. Time must be donated on a regular basis, usually for a period of three to six months and for a minimum of two days per week.

Nacro

Website: www.nacro.org.uk
Email: volunteering@nacro.org.uk
Tel: 020 7582 6500

Nacro is a charity that tries to find practical solutions to reducing crime by working with ex-offenders, disadvantaged people and deprived communities.

The charity's priorities are:

- resettling ex-offenders and prisoners
- mental health
- education and employment
- youth crime
- housing
- race and the criminal justice system

Its 200-plus projects may offer help to individuals, whole communities or organisations involved in reducing crime.

Specific projects include one-on-one support for young people in education and job-seeking, football coaching, mentoring for prisoners before and after release, and theatre and drama projects to help in mediating disputes between young people.

Volunteers can work in many different roles, often directly with individuals or groups. They are recruited from the area where the project is based. All volunteers are given a defined role, and receive training and support.

One Plus One

Website: www.oneplusone.org.uk
Email: kvsb@oneplusone.org.uk
Tel: 020 7553 9530

One Plus One is an organisation that focuses on how to help couples and families to avoid discord and break-up.

Founded by a psychiatrist, it conducts original research and monitors research across the UK and overseas. It produces videos and pamphlets for professionals and parents.

It also offers courses for professionals and volunteers who work on the frontline of family support but who are not counsellors, including GPs, health visitors, midwives, clergy, solicitors, police, teachers, or volunteers in Home-Start schemes. The training might cover:

- maternal postnatal depression
- the link between depression and relationship problems
- the effects of parental conflict on children

Volunteers are used in office work, in the library or in outreach.

Prisoners Abroad

Website: www.prisonersabroad.org.uk
Email: volunteer@prisonersabroad.org.uk
Tel: 020 7561 6581

Prisoners Abroad is a charity that helps British people who are imprisoned or detained overseas.

The charity offers advice, information and support to prisoners and their families or friends with the aim of safeguarding the prisoner's welfare and basic human rights. The charity helps those who have been convicted, regardless of the crime, and those who have not.

It also works with statutory and voluntary organisations to try to ensure that prisoners are not tortured or treated in an inhumane or degrading way, and it supports prisoners after they have been released.

Its services include an emergency fund for prisoners, which can be used for medical care, clothing, or special dietary needs not addressed by the prison. It sends prisoners books, magazines, educational materials and freepost letters. For the families, it may offer advice, telephone support, information on visiting, or financial aid for travel overseas.

Volunteers can work in many different roles. They can:

- help in the office
- raise funds
- become a pen pal to a prisoner
- send Christmas cards

No special skills are necessary, although those with a second language may be able to help to translate documents for a prisoner. Occasionally, volunteers can get involved in casework.

Prisoners' Families and Friends Service

Website: www.prisonersfamiliesandfriends.org.uk
Email: info@prisonersfamiliesandfriends.org.uk
Tel: 020 7403 4091 or 020 7403 9359

Prisoners' Families and Friends Service gives advice and support to prisoners' families and friends.

The service offers free confidential help and information for families or friends attending court, visiting a defendant or after a prisoner has been sentenced.

Volunteers are used to befriend and support the prisoners' close relatives and friends. Volunteers can also assist with court projects, working in the London Crown Courts or in various Magistrates' Courts one day a week. Court project volunteers advise and support the families when the prisoner is sentenced.

Royal National Lifeboat Institution

Website: www.rnli.org.uk
Email: info@rnli.org.uk
Tel: 0845 122 6999

The Royal National Lifeboat Institution, a charity, works to save lives at sea.

Its lifeboats provide a 24-hour search and rescue service up to 115 miles from the coast of the United Kingdom and Ireland. Since the institution was founded in 1824, its lifeboat crews have saved more than 137,000 people.

Almost 95% of the charity's 4,800 lifeboat crew members are volunteers. The charity also operates 62 lifeguard stations on beaches in south-west England. It relies on more than 30,000 volunteer fundraisers and 1,000 fundraising branches and guilds.

Volunteers can work as crew on lifeboats. No special skills are necessary. They can also act as lifeguards, on busy weekends and during holidays. Training is provided for both roles.

In addition, volunteers can work at fundraising events, or at individual branches in roles such as president, vice-president, chairperson, treasurer, secretary and souvenir secretary. Volunteers also assist in the charity's shops and museum.

Show Racism the Red Card

Website: www.srtrc.org
Email: info@theredcard.org
Tel: 0191 291 0160

Show Racism the Red Card is a charity that combats racism by using professional footballers as role models.

Part of a network entitled Football Against Racism in Europe, it uses education in the form of films, magazines, posters and educational packs to promote its message.

It also holds events and schools competitions. Hundreds of professional footballers and managers in Britain have been involved in the charity's campaign.

Volunteers can help to raise awareness, for example by assisting its education team with organising and holding workshops.

Soldiers, Sailors, Airmen and Families' Association Forces Help

Website: www.ssafa.org.uk
Email: info@ssafa.org.uk
Tel: 0845 1300 975

The Soldiers, Sailors, Airmen and Families' Association Forces Help, a charity, works with those who currently serve in the British armed forces, those who used to serve, and the families of both.

The charity's staff and its network of 7,000 volunteers deliver practical and financial assistance, emotional support, and health and numerous other services. It operates through 95 branches across the UK.

There is a small number of branches overseas. In addition, the charity serves communities of ex-service people in Ireland, Germany, Cyprus, Malta and Spain.

Volunteers' roles might include:

- providing childcare, social support or transport
- obtaining equipment for someone with a disability
- helping to fill in a form for social services, or applying to benefit agencies
- managing bills
- helping on one of the charity's holidays for service people, ex-service people or family members with special needs or a disability
- working in a local branch as publicity officers, treasurers, fundraisers, IT specialists and team leaders

St John Ambulance

Website: www.sja.org.uk
Tel: 08700 104950

St John Ambulance offers first aid assistance, training courses in first aid and lifesaving, and community programmes in health and safety.

The charity helps employers to assess workplace safety. It also offers more specialised services, such as first aid for the homeless or support to the elderly. At public events, it provides ambulances, first-aid and medical services.

It runs a National Schools First Aid Competition. Children between 5 and 10 years of age can join the Badgers, a group in which they learn about first aid and safety, while older children can become Cadets.

Volunteers can work in many roles:

- at public events
- by assisting with office-based work such as administration or PR
- by helping with catering

TimeBank
Time Together

Website: www.timetogether.org.uk

Time Together is a national project that aims to help refugees settle into their new community by matching them with UK citizens in one-to-one mentoring relationships. It is delivered in 24 locations across the UK in partnership with local organisations.

Mentors support, encourage, motivate and guide their mentee as they seek to achieve their goals in education, employment and integration. This involves spending about five hours a month with their mentee over a period of a year, sharing their knowledge and experience, and offering their friendship. This might mean doing anything from helping to write a CV, visiting a museum or art gallery, helping to practise English.

All mentors attend a one-day training course, are actively involved in selecting a suitable mentoring match and receive support and expenses for the duration of their mentoring relationship. Mentors must be over 18 years old, speak fluent English and either be British citizens or have lived in the UK long enough to have a real understanding of the culture and customs.

TimeBank
Volunteering Lives

Website: www.volunteeringlives.org.uk

Tel: 020 7785 6376

Volunteering Lives is a project in Waltham Forest, London, which helps people with learning disabilities to offer their services as volunteers.

The scheme offers people with learning disabilities a month-long volunteering placement doing something they are interested in. This might be anything from general office duties or gardening, to cooking or working with animals. They also have the option of a session support worker, who can offer guidance and assistance if needed.

Training For Life

Website: www.trainingforlife.org

Email: lorna@trainingforlife.org

Tel: 020 7444 4000

Training For Life is a charity that helps the unemployed to return to the workforce.

It runs social enterprises, personal development programmes and training courses that help people to overcome a variety of difficulties - such as with learning, reading or writing, the English language, computers, or a lack of confidence.

Courses are also offered on subjects such as hospitality, IT, customer service and administration, skills for life, and health and fitness.

Volunteers can help with the charity's mentor programme. A mentor usually spends time with an unemployed person who is interested in the mentor's field of work.

Women's Aid

Website: www.womensaid.org.uk
Email: info@womensaid.org.uk
Tel:01179 444411

Women's Aid is a charity working to help the victims of domestic violence.

It helps more than 320,000 women and children every year who face domestic violence, giving practical and emotional support. It offers education programmes, and with the charity Refuge, it runs a national helpline for those seeking help.

Women's Aid also advocates for abused women and children and attempts to increase their safety by influencing laws, policy and practice and working with key national and local agencies. It also tries to raise public awareness about domestic violence.

Volunteers can work on the telephone helpline, or help with fundraising.

DISABILITIES

Action for Blind People

Website: www.afbp.org

Email: humanresources@actionforblindpeople.org.uk

Tel: 020 7635 4800

Action for Blind People, a charity, works with blind and partially sighted people.

The charity, founded in 1857, aims to empower blind people. It offers support and advice to blind people, their families and friends on issues such as finding jobs, applying for benefits, housing and local services, using aids and adapting their environment.

It also works to make more jobs accessible to blind people, advises employers, and operates four hotels for the blind and partially sighted. Every year, the charity helps more than 22,000 people.

Volunteers can work in the charity's central office in London, in areas including:

- marketing
- fundraising
- information technology
- research
- support and advice
- helping the housing team

Volunteering opportunities outside London include:

- helping in children's activity clubs
- working at the charity's hotels
- providing information about the charity in local communities

Afasic

Website: www.afasic.org.uk

Email: info@afasic.org.uk

Tel: 020 7490 9410

Afasic, a parent-led organisation based in London, supports children and young people with speech and language impairments.

The organisation seeks to raise awareness and to improve services. It provides information and training for parents and professionals through local groups, its helpline and its publications. Afasic often works in partnership with local and national government, professional and statutory bodies and other voluntary organisations.

Volunteering opportunities include:

- helping with administration, mailings, fundraising and data input in the central office
- becoming a member of the trustee board
- assisting local groups with activities and events

Volunteers can also work on the helpline if they have relevant experience, such as having a child with a speech or language impairment. Training is offered, and volunteers are asked to make a regular commitment, for example, one day a week. Volunteer roles do not usually involve direct contact with children.

The Back-Up Trust

Website: www.backuptrust.org.uk
Email: admin@backuptrust.org.uk
Tel: 020 8875 1805

The Back-Up Trust is a charity that arranges outdoor activities and courses for people with a spinal cord injury.

A small organisation, the trust aims to encourage self-confidence, independence and motivation for people, old and young, with spinal injury. It also supports friends, families and colleagues.

The trust's courses range from skiing, sailing, kayaking and scuba diving to drama or wheelchair skills. The courses are held year-round and may last for one day, a weekend or a week.

The trust also organises trips for people with spinal injuries to visit hospitals to coach those who are recently injured in wheelchair skills across all terrains, including ramps, steps and kerbs.

In addition, it runs a mentoring programme that links up people with spinal injuries so that they can support each other. Its youth programme, for those under 18, matches able-bodied people with those who have a spinal injury for socialising and activities.

Opportunities for able-bodied volunteers include:

- youth mentoring
- helping during a course
- fundraising or organising events

Volunteers with spinal injuries can also work as mentors, trainers in wheelchair skills and youth visitors.

Choice Support

Website: www.choicesupport.org.uk
Email: Sarah.Maguire@choicesupport.org.uk
Tel: 020 7261 4103

Choice Support, a charity, provides services for adults with learning disabilities.

Its mission is to give people with learning disabilities as much control over their lives as possible.

The charity provides registered homes and supported living projects, outreach services, day activities, health programmes, housing management, and schemes to give work experience to those with a learning disability. Choice Support also offers a consultancy service.

Volunteers can help on the charity's One to One project, in which volunteers with a learning disability work alongside those who do not have one. The One to One projects are based in London, Aylesbury and Leicester.

Dial UK

Website: www.dialuk.org.uk
Email: enquiries@dialuk.org.uk
Tel: 01302 310 123

Dial UK is the national organisation for a network of advice centres run by and for disabled people.

It promotes the interests and use of local Disability Information and Advice Lines, or Dial centres, by providing them with information and support. The centres aim to ensure that every disabled person has access to specialist information and advice.

The network offers free advice on all aspects of disability to those who are disabled, their families and friends, carers and professionals. The advice is available over the telephone, during drop-by sessions at the centres or, for less mobile clients, through a home visit. The network's approximately 135 centres help a quarter of a million people yearly.

Volunteers need not be disabled. Possible roles at the head office or local branches include:

- general administration
- telephone reception
- data input and updating information
- marketing and fundraising
- information technology and training
- helping with the website

The Disabled Living Foundation

Website: www.dlf.org.uk
Email: info@dlf.org.uk
Tel: 020 7289 6111 or 020 7432 8004

The Disabled Living Foundation provides free advice on all types of equipment for disabled and older people.

A charity, it aims to help find equipment that enables disabled people to stay active and independent. The equipment might include stairlifts, walk-in baths, jar openers, tap turners, bath seats, walking sticks, wheelchairs, scooters, hoists and beds.

The foundation has a helpline service that answers telephone, letter and email enquiries about equipment and suppliers. The advice is available for the disabled, their families and carers.

The foundation also has a large centre for demonstrating equipment and runs a training programme for healthcare professionals. In addition, it offers an online tool that allows individuals to determine what equipment might help them, and an online database of available equipment.

Volunteers at the foundation are mostly office-based, working in reception or administration, accounting, basic research, marketing or fundraising. Volunteer healthcare professionals with experience in equipment can help to maintain up-to-date guides on equipment and answer email queries.

Elizabeth FitzRoy Support

Website: www.efitzroy.org.uk
Email: info@efitzroy.org.uk
Tel: 01730 711111

Elizabeth FitzRoy Support, a charity, provides practical support for adults with learning disabilities.

The charity, established in 1962, aims to help people with learning disabilities to develop to the best of their abilities, to make choices and participate in everyday life.

It offers a range of services around the UK, including:

- nursing and care homes for those with more need
- day support in the charity's own activity centres, such as classes in office and computer skills or swimming
- support for those in affordable housing

Those in nursing homes may have profound multiple disabilities. The care homes offer support for people with high levels of learning disability, very restricted mobility, sensory disabilities, or epilepsy and other medical conditions.

The charity helps approximately 500 people with learning disabilities and employs 800 full and part-time staff.

Volunteering opportunities are available in all of the charity's range of services, including such roles as driving, gardening, home visiting or as a lunch café assistant.

The Greater London Fund for the Blind

Website: www.glfb.org.uk
Email: info@glfb.org.uk
Tel: 020 7620 2066

The Greater London Fund for the Blind raises money for several member charities that help the blind.

The fund was established in 1921 to unify the collection of funds so that its members could focus on helping to improve the lives of visually impaired people in London.

Member charities range from the National Library for the Blind to local groups such as Croydon Voluntary Association for the Blind.

The fund raises money through the London Marathon and Geranium Day, when funds are collected across the city. Geranium Day is launched each year by the prime minister, who makes the first donation at 10 Downing Street.

Volunteers are needed to help in a geranium shop, in the head office or for Geranium Day.

Headway

Website: www.headway.org.uk
Email: enquiries@headway.org.uk
Tel: 0115 924 0800

Headway, based in Nottingham, is a charity that supports individuals affected by brain injury.

Every year, more than a million people attend hospital A&E departments in the UK following a head injury; around 135,000 of them will be admitted to a ward.

Headway offers local services through 110 local groups and branches. The services include programmes in rehabilitation and social reintegration, carer support, respite care and community outreach. The charity also helps to educate people about brain injury and the challenges faced by survivors and carers. It operates a national telephone helpline.

Volunteers can work in a variety of roles at the head office or at local branches. Opportunities include:

- answering helpline calls
- administrative assistance
- fundraising and communications
- helping brain injury survivors and carers
- working in the charity's shops

Training is given to volunteers on the helpline.

KeyRing

Website: www.keyring.org
Email: enquiries@keyring.org
Tel: 020 7749 9411

KeyRing is a charity that helps people with learning disabilities and other vulnerable individuals to live independently in their own homes.

The charity's aim is to create networks of support to empower those with learning disabilities and help them to interact in the community.

It operates communities consisting of about 10 properties within a 10-minute walk of each other. People who get support live in nine of the properties, and the tenth is for a volunteer. The volunteer supports the people with learning disability, encouraging them to help each other and to venture outside the network.

Volunteers, who offer 12 flexible hours a week, are given accommodation, training and support. No specific experience is necessary.

The Larches Trust

Website: www.larchestrust.org.uk
Email: enquiries@larchestrust.org.uk
Tel: 020 8905 6333

The Larches Trust, a small charity in Edgware, Middlesex, provides care and support for adults aged over 19 who have a learning disability.

Founded in 1995, the trust aims to provide education and support so that people with learning disabilities can become independent. It runs a leisure and recreation programme designed to foster socialising and community involvement.

The trust develops an individual plan for each person who is learning disabled. Its courses include: self-confidence and assertiveness; using public transport; numeracy; drama and movement; arts and crafts; computing; and how to take a holiday.

The trust also runs a support programme to help people with learning disabilities to participate in day-to-day activities such as going to the theatre or to a place of worship, having a meal out or going shopping.

Volunteers can work in a number of roles, including:

- helping with its art programme
- helping with various education programmes
- supporting people with learning disabilities in day-to-day activities
- helping with office-based tasks such as fundraising and marketing

Leonard Cheshire

Website: www.leonard-cheshire.org
Email: info@lc-uk.org
Tel: 020 7802 8200

Leonard Cheshire is a charity that supports disabled people.

The charity aims to offer choice, opportunity and independence to disabled people through services such as residential homes, home care, day services, resource centres, rehabilitation, respite care, personal support and training, and assistance for those looking for work.

The largest voluntary sector provider of care and support services for disabled people in the UK, it also seeks to change attitudes toward disability. The charity directly supports more than 21,000 disabled people in the UK and is active in an additional 51 countries.

Volunteers can work directly with disabled people, befriending or helping with transport, training and leisure activities. Other volunteers help by raising funds or by campaigning for disabled people. Volunteers may also work on the Discover IT programme, which enables disabled people to have access to computers and develop their IT skills.

You do not need any specific skills to become a volunteer; whatever your interests, Leonard Cheshire can put them to good use. The charity promotes diversity in volunteering and welcomes volunteer applications from all sections of the community.

The charity provides training for volunteers as well as a designated person to support each volunteer's activities, and it reimburses out-of-pocket expenses.

The Limbless Association

Website: www.limbless-association.org
Email: zafar@limbless-association.org
Tel: 020 8788 1777

The Limbless Association helps people who have lost one or more limbs to become independent.

The Association provides support to an individual in the home, in hospital, during rehabilitation, in education, employment and the community. Services are also available for the limbless person's family and carers.

Services include:

- a help bureau that offers advice to new and established amputees
- information on limb-fitting centres
- free legal advice
- home and hospital visits
- social programmes
- the Football+ programme, which gives children and young adults training in football; it also publishes a magazine, Step Forward.

The association helped victims who lost limbs during the 7/7 terrorist attack in London in 2005. In addition, it set up a fund to help children who lost limbs in the Iraq conflicts, which is named the Ali Fund for a 12-year-old boy who lost his entire family and both his arms.

Volunteers who have suffered limb loss themselves can become part of the association's network of volunteer visitors. These volunteers use their own practical experience to give advice and provide support to others.

Mencap

Website: www.mencap.org.uk
Email: volunteering@mencap.org.uk
Tel: 0845 123 3000

Mencap is a national learning disability charity working with people with a learning disability and their families and carers.

Mencap believes that people with a learning disability have an equal right to a life full of opportunities, from learning essential skills to securing paid employment. To this end, the charity campaigns for equal rights and provides a range of services to meet people's needs throughout their lives, including community support services, education and employment services and volunteering opportunities that enable people to achieve their goals

Volunteer activities are within Mencap, its affiliated groups and partner organisations. Roles with Mencap include:

- trustees
- advocates
- drivers
- befrienders
- sports and leisure club leaders and helpers

Out & About

Website: www.out-and-about.org.uk
Tel: 0870 770 5767

Out & About, a charity, helps disabled children and young people in Suffolk and Norfolk to become involved in activities and outings such as sports, cinema or youth clubs.

The charity believes that disabled children should have the same opportunities as their non-disabled peers, especially with regard to leisure.

It plans each child's activities with the children, their families and local leisure providers. Activities might include swimming, bowling, going to pubs and clubs and the cinema, guides and brownies, cubs and scouts, and after-school clubs. It caters for about 250 children.

Volunteers, who must be aged 16 or over, work with the children, helping them to participate in the activities.

RNID

Website: www.rnid.org.uk
Email: informationline@rnid.org.uk
Tel: 0808 808 0123 or 020 7296 8044

RNID is the largest British charity working with people who are deaf or hard of hearing.

It aims to help Britain's 9 million people with hearing loss through campaigning, information and support services, and by funding research into deafness, hearing loss and tinnitus.

The charity offers sign language interpreters and other communication support; career advice; telephone services; and equipment and products. It also teaches skills such as interpretation, speech-to-text operation, and basic sign language for organisations and businesses. It also operates a telephone helpline.

Volunteers can help with:

- campaigning, nationally or locally
- befriending people are starting to use hearing aids
- marketing
- research
- fundraising
- administration

The Royal National Institute of the Blind

Website: www.rnib.org.uk
Email: helpline@rnib.org.uk
Tel: 020 7388 1266

The Royal National Institute of the Blind (RNIB), a charity, works with people who are blind or partially blind.

The charity, offers information, support and advice to over two million people in Britain with sight problems. It also funds research and campaigns on issues such as making information or transport accessible.

Its services include projects that help people with sight problems to socialise, share information and support each other over the telephone. It also helps them to find and retain jobs. The charity has two colleges, in Loughborough and Redhill, that offer training for new careers.

The charity promotes products such as talking kitchen scales, calculators and watches, and magnifiers. Its transcription service works with companies and organisations to produce bills, statements, exam papers and magazines in formats such as large print, tape and braille.

Volunteering positions are available on more than 60 different projects, and guidance and training are offered. Volunteers can:

- work with blind and partially sighted people in their homes and communities or at

the charity's own facilities
- assist at events
- sell raffle tickets
- read books onto tape
- help with office work

Scope

Website: www.scope.org.uk
Email: volunteering@scope.org.uk
Tel: 0808 800 3333

Scope is a national disability charity with a focus on people with cerebral palsy.

Scope's services include face-to-face support at the point of diagnosis for parents; education and care for disabled children; ongoing support for the family; and employment and independent living services for disabled adults.

The organisation's Time to Get Equal campaign fights for equality and human rights for disabled people by lobbying government and challenging discriminatory attitudes in all areas of life.

Scope also runs Scope Response, which offers confidential advice and information about Scope's services, cerebral palsy or any aspect of living with disability.

Disabled people are encouraged to volunteer within the organisation, and Scope already has many disabled volunteers in its services, shops and mentoring roles across the country. Scope also urges other organisations to recruit disabled volunteers and provides advice about recruiting disabled volunteers.

Sense

Website: www.sense.org.uk/involved/volunteering
Email: info@sense.org.uk
Tel: 020 7561 3384

Sense, a national charity, supports and campaigns for children and adults who are deafblind.

Deafblindness is a combination of both sight and hearing difficulties. Deafblind people face major problems with communication, access to information and mobility. People can be born deafblind, or become deafblind through illness, accident or in older age.

Sense provides specialist information, advice and services to deafblind people, their families, carers and the professionals who work with them. In addition, they support people who have sensory impairments with additional disabilities.

Volunteers can be young and old, families and friends of deafblind people, interested supporters and people completely new to the work. In 2005/6 a total of 1,182 people volunteered for Sense, particularly:

- in the charity's network of shops
- on a holiday programme
- helping with a variety of fundraising events

The Spinal Injuries Association

Website: www.spinal.co.uk
Email: sia@spinal.co.uk
Tel: 0845 678 6633

The Spinal Injuries Association helps people with all levels of spinal cord injury.

The Association, founded in 1974, provides help and support to those with a spinal injury and to their family or friends. The injured person may be partially or fully paralysed.

Its services include a helpline, counselling, advisers on independent living, personal assistance and a newsletter. The Association operates a scheme that connects the injured people and their relatives with others, for support.

The Association also offers a travel fund for relatives who have to travel long distances to visit an injured relative. Its legal service helps with legal claims resulting from a spinal injury.

Volunteers can help:

- at fundraising events
- on the phoneline
- on support teams, visiting injured people at home or helping them by telephone
- volunteers who have spinal cord injuries themselves also can work in peer support

Vitalise

Website: www.vitalise.org.uk
Email: volunteer@vitalise.org.uk
Tel: 0845 330 0148

Vitalise, a charity, helps disabled people and carers by proving respite care and holidays.

The charity offers short breaks for disabled people aged 18-plus and their carers. Its centres are in Cornwall, Southampton, Essex, Nottingham and Southport. The centre in Cornwall takes children as young as six.

Each centre has a programme of activities, including excursions and entertainment, and volunteers who accompany guests to provide companionship and support. The centres hold more than 35 special interest holidays every year.

Vitalise also has centres in Cornwall and Derby that provide day support as well as programmes that aim to promote independence.

For visually impaired people, the charity organises holidays in the UK and overseas. Each holiday is focused on a specific city or activity. A volunteer sighted guide accompanies each group.

Volunteers need no special experience. Opportunities for volunteering include:

- helping for a week at one of the residential centres
- accompanying visually impaired people on the city breaks and activity holidays
- helping in an office or shop

Training and support are provided, and all meals and accommodation at Vitalise centres are free.

Whizz-Kidz

Website: www.whizz-kidz.org.uk
Email: info@whizz-kidz.org.uk
Tel: 020 7233 6600

Whizz-Kidz is a charity that works with disabled children and young people who need customised mobility equipment such as wheelchairs and tricycles.

The group provides funding for a broad range of mobility equipment for under-18s that may not be available through the National Health Service.

These include powered, manual and sports wheelchairs, and specially adapted tricycles, bicycles, buggies and walking aids. The charity has funded equipment for more than 4,500 young disabled people.

It also offers information, training and advice on wheelchairs and has a small network of mobility therapists. It has a wheelchair training scheme and a mobility centre for information and advice. The charity also works to raise awareness of issues such as why some children need customised mobility equipment.

Volunteers can help with:

- fundraising
- raising awareness locally by giving talks to groups and events and the media
- general administration

ENVIRONMENT

Blue Ventures

Website: www.blueventures.org
Email: volunteer@blueventures.org
Tel: 020 8341 9819

Blue Ventures, a charity, works to conserve marine resources and the communities that rely upon them.

The charity believes that environmental protection and economic development cannot be separated.

Blue Ventures is involved in regional conservation and educational initiatives around the world. It coordinates expeditions in the UK and overseas in which its scientists and volunteers work with local biologists, government departments, non-governmental organisations and local communities.

The teams conduct research, boost environmental awareness and conserve marine habitats. Expeditions are held year-round and usually last for six weeks, although longer and shorter trips are available.

In one major project, the charity is developing a community-run protected area in a remote fishing village, Andavadoaka, in south-west Madagascar. In 2004, Blue Ventures volunteers and staff helped Andavadoaka establish the world's first community-run protected area for octopus. The charity is also building an eco-tourism lodge and helping villagers to develop the farming of algae, seagrass and sea cucumber.

Volunteers can work on the project in Andavadoaka, researching and assisting with conservation. No special skills are needed. Training is provided, including in scuba diving. Other opportunities in Andavadoaka include monitoring baobab forests and mangrove, helping with sea farming or teaching English to local children.

BTCV

Website: www.btcv.org
Email: information@btcv.org.uk
Tel: 01302 388 888

BTCV, a practical conservation charity, works to improve the environment through local conservation action across the UK and overseas.

The charity supports local teams of volunteers who undertake one-day conservation projects such as planting trees and bulbs, dry stone walling, creating and maintaining footpaths and maintaining woodland and grassland.

Its Green Gym™ programme encourages people to get fit through the same type of conservation work, using traditional hands-on techniques rather than labour-saving machinery.

BTCV organises more than 200 conservation holidays yearly in the UK and abroad. Every year, about 130,000 volunteers work on BTCV projects. The charity also offers training opportunities, from practical conservation to conservation management.

Volunteers can work on any of the projects. They need have no special skills and are supervised by a trained project leader.

Earthwatch

Website: www.earthwatch.org
Email: info@earthwatch.org.uk
Tel: 01865 318838

Earthwatch, an international charity, supports long-term field research that addresses environmental problems.

The charity aims to improve understanding of critical environmental issues. It manages 130 conservation projects in more than 50 countries by providing scientists with both funding and volunteers.

The research ranges from gathering information about the impact of climate change or monitoring the habitat needs of endangered species, to finding solutions to land conflicts between wildlife and local communities.

In St Croix, in the Virgin Islands, Earthwatch volunteers have patrolled turtle nesting beaches for 25 years, moving the eggs above the high-tide mark to minimise poaching. As a result, the number of turtles hatched has increased twenty-fold.

Volunteers of any age, alone or in groups, can participate in the projects. They must pay to join an expedition, to cover the costs of the research and their travel, accommodation, food, training, plans for medical evacuation and the offsetting of greenhouse gas emissions from travel. Expeditions usually last from two days to three weeks. No special skills are required, unless the project involves diving.

ENCAMS

Website: www.encams.org
Tel: 01942 612621

ENCAMS is the independent charity behind the campaign Keep Britain Tidy.

The charity aims to improve the areas where people work, live and socialise by making them clean and safe. Its campaigns are specifically designed to encourage people to stop littering or dumping junk and to stop graffiti.

It offers information and guidance for groups that want to clean up their communities. It also looks after UK programmes such as the Blue Flag awards for clean beaches and the international campaign for pupils, Eco-Schools, which encourages children to think about how their day-to-day actions affect the environment.

Volunteers can participate by:

- picking up litter
- assisting with the charity's campaigning
- helping with the schools programme

Green & Away

Website: www.greenandaway.org
Email: mike@greenandaway.org
Tel: 01684 893380

Green & Away operates Europe's only environmentally sustainable outdoor conference centre each summer at its site in Worcestershire.

Its aim is to support voluntary and campaigning organisations by providing facilities built to a high environmental standard which inspire and re-energise the participants. The centre can accommodate 100 to 150 participants and is used by organisations such as Friends of the Earth.

The centre, which consists of tents and other canvas structures in the form of a small village, serves locally grown organic food and uses renewable energy, composting toilets and wood-burning water-heating systems.

Volunteers work on-site during the season (July–August). Opportunities include:

- helping to build the centre (marquees, yurts, benders, field kitchen, bar)
- cooking
- gardening
- washing up
- looking after children
- arts and crafts activities
- welcoming people
- office work
- maintaining the site

GreenNet

Website www.gn.apc.org
Email: info@gn.apc.org
Tel: 0845 055 4011

GreenNet is an internet service provider for groups and individuals working for the environment, peace and human rights.

A not-for-profit collective established in 1986, it offers email and internet connection, website hosting and design, and training and consultancy.

It also provides an international gateway for small, indigenous networks in Africa and Asia. Any profits go to the GreenNet Educational Trust to support and promote the use of information and communication technology among small and medium-sized groups, especially non-governmental organisations.

Volunteers can help with any aspect of GreenNet's services, including the GreenNet Educational Trust.

Groundwork

Website: www.groundwork.org.uk
Email: info@groundwork.org.uk
Tel: 0121 236 8565

Groundwork is a federation of trusts that helps to reclaim underused land, makes environmental improvements, builds sports facilities and creates green space.

Its goal is to build sustainable communities in deprived areas, thus improving the lives of local people and the local economy with a cleaner, safer and greener environment.

Groundwork's programmes are administered by experienced professionals who aim to create stronger neighbourhoods, reconnect people with their surroundings, train individuals for work, stimulate enterprise, and integrate the economy with environmental goals.

The federation works closely with the UK government, both domestically and on global sustainable development and avoiding climate change.

Volunteering opportunities vary tremendously. No special skills are necessary, but in some cases the work is especially suitable for volunteers who are seeking a career in the environmental field or economic regeneration.

Kent Wildlife Trust

Website: www.kentwildlifetrust.org.uk
Email: info@kentwildlife.org.uk
Tel: 01622 662012

Kent Wildlife Trust, founded in 1958, is one of the largest of 47 wildlife trusts across the UK, and works to ensure a better future for both Kent's wildlife and its people.

The organisation manages more than 59 nature reserves covering 3,035-plus hectares, and it seeks to influence government policies that affect wildlife habitats across Kent.

It also has a wildlife awareness programme that reaches some 25,000 children and adults yearly. The Trust is supported by more than 27,000 members and 1,000 volunteers.

Opportunities for volunteer involvement include:

- assisting at visitor centres
- managing nature reserves
- helping children and adults to value and understand wildlife
- working to raise the profile of wildlife conservation

Volunteers aged under 16 must work alongside a parent or guardian. Some roles require good communication skills or specialised knowledge, but most just need enthusiasm and a willingness to learn.

The Marine Conservation Society

Website: www.mcsuk.org
Email: info@mcsuk.org
Tel: 01989 566017

The Marine Conservation Society (MCS) is a charity that works to protect the UK's seas, shores and marine wildlife.

The charity's mission is to secure clean seas and beaches, sustainable fisheries and the protection of marine life and habitats. It also raises awareness through education and community involvement and tries to encourage action by individuals, industry and government to protect the marine environment.

The UK has more than 18,470 km of coastline. MCS arranges fundraising events in which sponsored participants walk along their favourite stretch of coastline, or simply add up miles on a treadmill.

It compiles sightings of marine species - such as basking sharks, turtles and jellyfish - around UK shores. It also monitors beaches for litter and pollution so that the most common sources are identified.

Volunteers can help to clean up beaches on a quarterly or annual basis, raise funds or participate in a wide range of other projects.

With the appropriate diving qualification, volunteers can help to conduct Seasearch surveys, identifying and monitoring marine wildlife. Training for Seasearch is available.

The National Trust

Website: www.nationaltrust.org.uk
Email: enquiries@thenationaltrust.org.uk
Tel: 0870 458 4000

The National Trust, a charity, works to preserve and protect the countryside, the coastline and historic buildings and gardens.

Founded by three volunteers more than a century ago, it now looks after 250,000 hectares of countryside, 1,100 miles of coastline and hundreds of buildings that are visited by more than 60 million people yearly.

The Trust has nearly 3.5 million members and 43,000 volunteers.

It offers more than 180 different roles for volunteers, ranging from booksellers to bricklayers, carpenters to caretakers, gardeners to gatekeepers, mechanics to musicians, ornithologists to organisers. Volunteers may be able to work towards a qualification.

Volunteers can also participate in a working holiday, which often involves outdoor work. The Trust works with businesses so that groups of volunteers can donate time together.

Plantlife

Website: www.plantlife.org.uk
Email: enquiries@plantlife.org.uk
Tel: 01722 342730

Plantlife is a charity that works to preserve Britain's wild plants and their habitats.

It aim is to protect plants, ranging from flowers to lichens, from habitat destruction, invasive plants from overseas, over-grazing, climate change and pollution.

The charity carries out practical field work with rare species, buys land for its nature reserves, and encourages people to get involved in its surveys and workdays.

The charity seeks to influence UK and international policy and environmental laws. It also commissions research and publishes reports to raise awareness. Its international team works to protect wild plants and their habitats overseas, in areas ranging from alpine meadows to the Central American rainforest.

Volunteers can work in the field, helping with conservation, at a nature reserve or by monitoring endangered plants. No prior experience is necessary.

Plantlife also uses volunteers in its office in Salisbury. The work usually involves a commitment of one day a week. Computer skills are not required but are desirable.

Royal Horticultural Society

Website: www.rhs.org.uk
Email: info@rhs.org.uk
Tel: 0845 260 5000

The Royal Horticultural Society works to advance horticulture and to promote good gardening.

The charity conducts research, owns gardens, holds flower shows, offers advice and organises more than 1,000 lectures and demonstrations yearly throughout the UK. Its members receive a monthly magazine, The Garden.

Volunteers do not need special skills. They may:

- work as stewards at the gardens and assist visitors
- log the details of plantings or maintain borders
- help to recruit new members
- help in the charity's libraries and reading rooms

Sustrans

Website: www.sustrans.org.uk
Email: info@sustrans.org.uk
Tel: 0845 113 0065

Sustrans is a charity that works to promote sustainable transport.

Its mission is to give people a choice of transport, both public and private, that benefits their health and the environment.

It operates a number of projects and programmes, including a national cycle network and the TravelSmart scheme, which gives individual households the information they need to be able to walk, cycle and use public transport more.

Sustrans works within the education system, collaborating with young people and schools to encourage safe cycling and walking. It offers a community scheme that implements practical projects that seek to combine urban design, community involvement and the planning of sustainable transport.

It also has an art and landscape programme, which commissions artworks - such as sculptures, mileposts, seats and drinking fountains - to create more memorable public spaces.

Volunteers can work as rangers for the national cycle network, putting up signs or clearing the paths. In addition, volunteers are used to help promote Sustrans at events and exhibitions, participate in summer work camps or assist with administration at the charity's office in Bristol.

Thames Explorer

Website: www.thames-explorer.org.uk
Email: info@thames-explorer.org.uk
Tel: 020 8742 0057

Thames Explorer, an environmental and educational charity, works to improve access to the River Thames.

It aims to enable all types of people, including the young, disadvantaged and disabled, to visit and learn about the Thames.

The charity provides a wide range of programmes including:

- river visits for schools, community groups and adults
- training for teachers, youth leaders and staff of other Thames-related organisations
- publication of educational materials about the whole Thames Basin
- consultancy on issues relating to the Thames

The charity has organised visits for children with learning difficulties or disabilities. Thames Explorer also works with other groups such as the Thames Education Network, the Environment Agency and the Thames Estuary Partnership to plan for the river's future.

Contact Thames Explorer for information about volunteering opportunities.

Thames21

Website: www.thames21.org.uk/
Email: info@thames21.org.uk
Tel: 020 7248 7171

Thames21 is an environmental charity that works to protect and improve rivers and canals in London.

Its aim is to benefit the environment, protect wildlife habitats and encourage Londoners to use and respect their waterways. Every year, the charity works with more than 4,000 volunteers.

The charity's major projects are:

- Project Habitat, in which research and testing is being done on ways to improve biodiversity on the River Thames in central London
- Tightlines, in which angling is used to tackle anti-social behaviour among young people, who are also encouraged to become stewards of their waterways

In addition the organisation is sponsoring Haggerston Breathing Places to help people in Hackney to clean up and improve a section of the Regent's Canal.

Volunteers are needed to work on waterways by cleaning up litter and graffiti, by identifying problem stretches of the river or canal, and by reporting wildlife in trouble.

Volunteers can also work on the charity's Adopt-a-River scheme, which enables local groups and businesses to look after a stretch of river and help to keep it clean. Thames21 provides equipment and backup, including disposal of litter, and helps organisers to publicise their activities locally.

Yorkshire Wildlife Trust

Website: www.yorkshire-wildlife-trust.org.uk
Email: info@yorkshirewt.cix.co.uk
Tel: 01904 659570

Yorkshire Wildlife Trust works to protect vulnerable wildlife and wildlife habitats.

Its aim is to preserve habitats and species of animals or plants that might otherwise be lost. The Trust oversees more than 80 nature reserves in rural and urban Yorkshire, some of which include threatened species such as otters and water voles.

It also tries to encourage communities to protect and enjoy wildlife through education. Wildlife Watch groups give young people aged 8 to 16 the chance to learn about nature. Landowners are offered advice on how to manage their land in a way that benefits wildlife.

Volunteers can work outdoors on practical conservation projects. They can also work with young people, assist at events or help with PR and publicity.

The Wilderness Foundation

Website: www.wildernessfoundation.org.uk
Email: info@wildernessfoundation.org.uk
Tel: 0124 544 3073

The Wilderness Foundation helps to protect wilderness world-wide, often in conjunction with similar organisations overseas.

To reach its goal of conserving wilderness, it educates people about the environmental benefits of wild places, provides opportunities for people to experience them and campaigns for their preservation.

In addition, the Foundation offers education and youth support programmes in Britain, South Africa and elsewhere. The programmes are intended to increase awareness as well as to foster leadership skills and personal development.

Internationally, the Foundation works closely with the Wilderness Foundation in South Africa, the WILD Foundation in the US, and groups in Europe and Asia.

Volunteers can help on a wide variety of projects. Opportunities might include working on game reserves or marine research projects in South Africa, or helping to establish eco-tourism on an island in Norway.

Placements vary in length. In Africa, placements range from four to 12 weeks, during which volunteers may help with anti-poaching patrols, monitoring wildlife, darting and animal capture, bush restoration and day-to-day maintenance of the reserve.

No experience or qualification is required for most roles, although some posts - such as supporting scientists working on the reserves - are only suitable for science students.

The Wildfowl & Wetlands Trust

Website: www.wwt.org.uk
Email: enquiries@wwt.org.uk
Tel: 01453 891900

The Wildfowl & Wetlands Trust works to conserve wetlands -- including rivers, ponds, bogs, fens, marshes and estuaries -- and to protect wetland wildlife.

Founded in 1946 by the artist and naturalist Sir Peter Scott, it both saves and restores wetlands, and protects threatened animals such as ducks, geese, swans and flamingos, as well as plants. The trust offers programmes in recreation and education at its nine wetland visitor centres across the UK.

Its environmental specialists consult on areas important to wetland and wildlife conservation, including ecological surveying, wetland habitat design, eco-hydrology, visitor centre planning and fostering links between wildlife and people.

Volunteers can work at the wetland centres, providing support and help to visitors, and on educational and recreational programmes.

The Wildlife Trusts

Website: www.wildlifetrusts.org
Email: enquiry@wildlifetrusts.org
Tel: 0870 036 7711

The charity Wildlife Trusts is made up of a group of local organisations that are dedicated to conserving the full range of habitats and wildlife in the UK.

Their mission is to re-introduce biodiversity and engage people with their environment. The 47 local trusts are voluntary organisations with a total of 670,000 members.

The trusts manage 2,200 nature reserves. They also operate projects to help young people to explore their local environment and are involved in community gardening, surveying species of animals and plants, and outdoor programmes to encourage fitness.

Volunteers can work outdoors, helping at the nature reserves, with young people or on fitness programmes. Other opportunities include assisting with organisation, IT, administration and finance.

The Woodland Trust

Website: www.woodland-trust.org.uk
Email: enquiries@woodland-trust.org.uk
Tel: 01476 581 135

The Woodland Trust works on protecting the UK's native woodlands.

The Trust conserves lands with trees or shrubs by acquiring, restoring and protecting it. It oversees the planting and conservation of native trees and shrubs at other sites. And it lobbies the government, landowners and other groups to try to protect and expand Britain's woods.

Since the Trust's founding in 1972, it has grown to care and protect over 1,100 sites covering 19,000 hectares. This ranges from sites of national and international significance to small urban or village woods.

Volunteers can help by planting trees, arranging a talk for a local group, or helping to conduct surveys and mapping the UK's ancient trees.

HEATH AND SOCIAL CARE

Action against Medical Accidents

Website: www.avma.org.uk
Email: advice@avma.org.uk
Tel: 020 8667 9065

Action against Medical Accidents, a charity, gives advice to people harmed by medical treatment.

Medical accidents, whether caused by negligence or not, can also occur because of failure to treat a person appropriately.

The charity aims to help those who have been injured to get an explanation, support and, if appropriate, compensation. It also seeks to ensure that necessary steps will be taken to prevent similar medical accidents. The charity runs a helpline and publishes leaflets on a variety of related topics.

Its team of medically and legally trained caseworkers provide free, confidential advice on patients' rights. They also offer medical information; help in investigating the issues; assessment of the likelihood of obtaining compensation; referral to an appropriate solicitor for individual cases; and other practical and emotional support.

Volunteers can fill a variety of roles, including working on the helpline or fundraising.

Addaction

Website: www.addaction.org.uk
Email: info@addaction.org.uk
Tel: 020 7251 5860

Addaction, a charity, provides treatment for drug and alcohol abuse.

Founded in 1967, it has more than 70 centres across the UK, from Glasgow to Penzance. It treats clients of any age and from all socio-economic backgrounds.

The charity assesses an individual client's needs and helps them to stop drinking or taking drugs. Clients often require several types of support.

The charity's day programmes provide counselling, therapy and medication, family support and intervention. In some areas, it offers training in job skills, and helps with employment and with housing problems. Addaction also runs projects involving outreach, including to those in prison and those just arrested.

It has needle-exchange programmes to help to minimise the spread of infectious diseases such as hepatitis and HIV. And it runs the Smart scheme, which offers professional training in London to help employers cope with the long-term problems in planning their workforce because of substance misuse.

Volunteers can work in hands-on roles, including in the Smart scheme. Volunteers receive on-the-job training. They may work towards a National Vocational

Qualification in health and social services. Addaction also offers a number of other training programmes around the country.

After Adoption

Website: www.afteradoption.org.uk
Email: information@talkadoption.org.uk
Tel: 0161 839 4932

After Adoption works with anyone whose life has been affected by adoption – children, families or adults – to offer support throughout the adoption process.

This can involve helping a birth relative to deal with loss, helping all parties involved to search for a relative, or providing counselling and information to adoptive families, birth relatives and adopted people.

It provides two national telephone helplines, where trained telephone counsellors offer information, advice and support:

- ActionLine for adults
- TALKadoption for young people

It has a family finding service, 'Families that Last,' which places children with adoptive families. The service works with particularly 'hard to place' young children, the majority of whom have had unstable lives. It supports new families through the adoption process, working towards the stability needed to embrace a happier future.

Volunteers provide information, advice and support around adoption. They do not need to be qualified social workers or counsellors, as volunteers also provide help in administration, finance, fundraising and communications. All volunteers are trained, supported and supervised, and all agreed out-of-pocket expenses are reimbursed.

Alzheimer's Society

Website: www.alzheimers.org.uk
Email: enquiries@alzheimers.org.uk
Tel: 020 7306 0606

The Alzheimer's Society, a charity, works with people with dementia and their carers.

The charity aims to provide help and support and to raise awareness about dementia. It also funds medical and scientific research into Alzheimer's and related diseases, and campaigns for improved health and social services.

Its services include support for carers, and day and home care. It publishes fact sheets and has a helpline and support groups. The charity provides training for healthcare professionals and service providers.

The Alzheimer's Society is a membership organisation that operates through a partnership between the national organisation and 250 branches and support groups across England, Wales and Northern Ireland.

Volunteers can work at the charity's local branches.

Arthritis Care

Website: www.arthritiscare.org.uk
Email: info@arthritiscare.org.uk
Tel: 020 7380 6500

Arthritis Care works for people with arthritis by providing information and support.

Founded in 1947, it also aims to raise awareness of the condition and influence decision-makers to provide better services.

It publishes information; operates free helplines; runs self-management courses; and encourages support groups and discussion.

Volunteering opportunities are centred on three main areas:

- information
- campaigning
- training

Volunteers can assist with publications or campaigning, give courses or run workshops, or help with support groups and discussions.

Volunteers generally contribute between two and ten hours flexitime per month. However, volunteers who offer courses and workshops must commit to a set timetable over a period of several weeks.

Asthma UK

Website: www.asthma.org.uk
Email: info@asthma.org.uk
Tel: 020 7786 5000 or 020 7786 4900

Asthma UK is a charity working with people who have asthma.

The charity aims to improve the health of people who have asthma. It offers help to their carers and healthcare professionals.

It funds nearly £3 million of research into the disease yearly, helps to disseminate research, and provides information to local groups, schools and clubs or during health awareness days and festivals.

The charity also offers Kick Asthma, a programme of adventure holidays for young people and children. The holidays combine physical and social activities, such as abseiling, kayaking, discos and quizzes, with educational sessions to teach youngsters more about controlling asthma.

Volunteers can help by:

- giving talks
- promotion
- campaigning
- assisting at the week-long adventure holidays

BackCare

Website: www.backcare.org.uk
Email: membership@backcare.org
Tel: 020 8977 5474

BackCare, a charity, is a support network for people who have chronic back pain.

Also known as the National Back Pain Association, the charity consists of 20 local support groups run by volunteers. At a national level, BackCare produces information, campaigns and runs a helpline.

The local branches, in partnership with health professionals and therapists, offer such programmes as pain management and exercise. In addition, they organise hydrotherapy sessions, workshops and other activities.

Volunteers can help:

W at local branches by working in the office, where tasks might include obtaining advertisements for the members' magazine, stuffing envelopes, or doing data entry and sending out publications

W volunteers with counselling skills or a health background can work on the telephone helpline, which is overseen by nurses

Bell's Palsy Association

Website: www.bellspalsy.org.uk
Email: enquiries@bellspalsy.org.uk
Tel: 0870 44 45 46 0

Bell's Palsy Association is a small charity that works with people who have Bell's palsy, which causes facial paralysis.

The charity's primary aim is to provide information to the sufferer and their families. Every year, between 25,000 and 100,000 people develop Bell's palsy, a condition that is usually temporary.

Volunteers can help with fundraising and promotion.

Black Health Agency

Website: www.blackhealthagency.org.uk
Email: info@blackhealthagency.org.uk
Tel: 0845 450 4247

Black Health Agency (BHA), a charity and social enterprise based in Manchester, works with black and minority ethnic and other marginalised communities to improve their health and wellbeing.

The charity offers a range of services to diverse communities locally, regionally and nationally. It also raises awareness about the health needs of black and minority ethnic communities through policy and training.

Its services include:

- a free, multilingual helpline providing information about HIV/Aids to Africans living in the UK
- a support service for black and minority ethnic people in Greater Manchester living with or affected by HIV
- family support services for international new arrivals and mental health support for refugees and those seeking asylum
- a peer education project for young black men and women on such issues as sexual health, parenting, drugs and alcohol, self-esteem, and training and employment
- a project targeting South Asian women's health issues
- an initiative providing culturally sensitive drugs and alcohol awareness education to minority ethnic communities in Manchester

For details of these and other projects visit the website.

Volunteers do not need special skills, neither do they need to be from a minority ethnic background. Volunteers can work on topics such as HIV, young people's issues or drugs and alcohol. They can also work in finance, event organisation, marketing, fundraising and PR.

The Blood Pressure Association

Website: www.bpassoc.org.uk

Tel: 020 8772 4994

The Blood Pressure Association, a charity, works to help people who have high blood pressure.

The charity provides information on issues such as medication, home monitoring and lifestyle changes. It aims to educate and make blood pressure a priority both for individuals, especially those who are at high risk, and for the government.

It also tries to improve the detection, monitoring, management and treatment of the illness. It provides healthcare professionals with literature developed specifically to help patients, and it disseminates information about the latest developments in hypertension and how it may affect healthcare practice.

Volunteers can help in the charity's offices in London. Those with specialist skills can work in finance, PR, marketing or fundraising. Volunteers can also help to raise awareness in their local area or raise funds through local events.

Breast Cancer Campaign

Website: www.breastcancercampaign.org

Email: volunteer@breastcancercampaign.org

Tel: 020 7749 3700 or 020 7749 3708

Breast Cancer Campaign is a charity specialising in funding independent breast cancer research throughout the UK.

It aims to find a cure for breast cancer by funding research on diagnosis and treatment of the disease, on how it develops, and on curing or preventing it. Over the past 11 years, the charity has spent more than £14.5 million on research.

Volunteers can help to campaign, raise funds or improve public awareness. Specifically, they can organise sponsored walks or supermarket collections, or become a spokesperson for the charity.

The Campaign has a volunteer pack, which includes details of possible volunteering roles, plus fundraising tips and suggestions. The pack can be downloaded from the website or mailed.

British Heart Foundation

Website: www.bhf.org.uk

Tel: 020 7935 0185

The British Heart Foundation, a charity, fights against heart disease by supporting heart patients and funding research and education.

The charity seeks to help people to lower the risk of dying prematurely from a heart-related disease.

It is the largest independent funder of heart research in the UK. It also funds education for the public and for health professionals, and it provides cardiac equipment and support for rehabilitation and patient care.

More than 2.6 million people in the UK have coronary heart disease, the biggest cause of premature death in the country.

Volunteers can help with local fundraising or by assisting in the foundation's shops. Specialist skills are required for some roles including:

- coordinating campaigns in schools
- identifying and valuing donated books, music, designer clothing, antiques and jewellery
- handling and acknowledging donations left as memorials

Volunteers can also donate time during the annual fundraising campaigns, in February or June.

The British Lung Foundation

Website: www.lunguk.org

Tel: 08458 50 50 20

The British Lung Foundation is a charity that works with people who have lung disease.

The charity seeks to support those with any type of lung disease, from mild asthma to lung cancer. It has a national network of support groups for those who have lung disease or who are parents of children with lung disease.

The Foundation, started by a group of medical specialists in lung disease, provides educational information by telephone, in pamphlets and online. The volunteer-staffed helpline, based in Liverpool, receives calls from about 10,000 people a year.

In addition, the Foundation works to improve lung health by campaigning, raising awareness and funding research. The British Lung Foundation has six offices throughout the UK.

Volunteers can help at the Breathe Easy support groups, which are usually held monthly and run by patients or by parents. Volunteers can also help to raise awareness, raise funds, organise speakers or do administrative work.

The British Red Cross

Website: www.redcross.org.uk
Email: information@redcross.org.uk
Tel: 0870 170 7000

The British Red Cross is a member of a global humanitarian network – the International Red Cross and Red Crescent Movement.

It is a charity that responds to disasters and conflicts around the world and helps fellow Red Cross and Red Crescent societies to cope with emergencies and day-to-day aid in their own countries. It also tries to reunite those separated by war or disaster.

The focal point of the charity's overseas operations is its international aid department, based in London.

In addition, it helps vulnerable people, such as the homeless, to prepare for and deal with emergencies in their own communities. And it offers services across the UK such as first aid, and care and transport for those with health problems.

Volunteers can work for the Red Cross in many communities in Britain by:

- responding to emergencies
- helping vulnerable people
- assisting in its shops
- giving first-aid training
- providing first aid at events
- delivering refugee services
- offering transport and support for fire and emergency personnel

Brook Advisory Centres

Website: www.brook.org.uk
Email: admin@brookcentres.org.uk
Tel: 020 7284 6040

Brook Advisory Centres provide free and confidential sexual health advice and services for young people under 25 years old.

Brook, as it is commonly known, is a registered charity. It has 40 years' experience of giving advice through specialist doctors, nurses, counsellors, and outreach and information workers. It works with more than 100,000 young people each year.

It offers the advice through a network of 17 centres across the UK. In addition to advice, the centres provide contraception, education and related services if needed.

The Brook central office in London oversees the network and provides advocacy, campaigning, communications and policy work. It seeks to educate opinion formers and the public about young people's sexual health and to encourage open discussion.

The charity's information service also operates a freephone helpline and an email enquiry service. It produces publications on sexual health issues for young people, teachers, parents and youth workers.

Volunteers can work at different levels, as trustees, as part of peer support programmes and in official posts at the centres.

Cancer Research UK

Website: www.cancerresearchuk.org
Tel: 020 7242 0200

Cancer Research UK is a charity that supports research on all aspects of cancer through the work of more than 3,000 scientists, doctors and nurses.

The charity seeks to improve understanding of the disease and to develop better ways to prevent, diagnose and treat it.

In addition to supporting research, it provides information to cancer patients and their families, the general public and health professionals. The organisation also works with the government to ensure that cancer is prioritised in the national health agenda.

Volunteers can assist in the charity's 600 shops, located across the UK. At the charity's two head offices and 17 local offices, volunteers can also donate their professional skills or expertise.

In addition, volunteers can help to run one of the charity's fundraising events, such as 10K runs and bicycle rides.

The Chinese Mental Health Association

Website: www.cmha.org.uk
Email: info@cmha.org.uk
Tel: 020 7613 1008

The Chinese Mental Health Association, a charity, offers community-based mental health services to the Chinese community in the United Kingdom.

The charity aims to encourage people of Chinese descent to access mental health services despite barriers that can arise from the stigma of mental health, especially in traditional Chinese society.

Its services include providing medical information, counselling and advice. It has a helpline and publishes printed information about mental health in Chinese.

Volunteers can work with individuals, offering support, or on the helpline. Trainee counsellors can volunteer to provide counselling.

There are also opportunities to volunteer on the charity's Chinese oral history project. Tasks might include interviewing and recording the Chinese older generation. Camera operators, video and film editors, producers, researchers, translators and graphic designers are needed for the oral history project.

Crusaid

Website: www.crusaid.org.uk
Email: office@crusaid.org.uk
Tel: 020 7539 3880

Crusaid is a charity that works with poor and marginalised people affected by HIV and Aids in the UK and Africa.

The charity provides grants and funding for individuals, projects and research. It aims to ensure that the money disbursed has the maximum impact in the fight against the disease.

Specifically, it provides grants from a hardship fund to poor people in Britain who have HIV or Aids. It also funds projects in Britain and Africa that offer information, education and services to support people with HIV. The projects range from outpatient clinics to back-to-work projects. The charity also funds research on new treatments for HIV and Aids.

Volunteers can help in the office, in its charity shop, or helping to organise fundraising events such as Walk for Life.

Depression Alliance

Website: www.depressionalliance.org
Email: information@depressionalliance.org
Tel: 0845 123 23 20

Depression Alliance, a charity, works to help people with depression.

The charity aims to encourage people to seek treatment and support as soon as possible, and to raise awareness about the illness.

It provides information and assistance to those who are affected by depression through publications and education. It offers training, support to individuals, and consultancy. It oversees a network of more than 60 self-help groups, many of them run by volunteer group coordinators.

The alliance also works with government agencies and healthcare professionals to improve services for people with depression. It seeks to publicise the illness by organising various events and initiatives, including Depression Awareness Week.

Volunteers can work:

- as coordinators for self-help groups
- by starting new groups in counties where there are none
- in fundraising

Eating Disorders Association

Website: www.edauk.com
Email: info@edauk.com
Tel: 0870 770 3256

Eating Disorders Association, a charity, provides information, help and support for people affected by eating disorders.

Founded in 1989, the charity primarily focuses on anorexia and bulimia nervosa. It maintains national telephone helplines; has a UK-wide network of self-help and support groups and contacts; and issues lists of treatment available around the country.

It disseminates information on eating disorders, including leaflets for young people, and training and publications for healthcare professionals. The charity's professional journal, European Eating Disorders Review, offers information and practical help for professionals in all disciplines. It also sponsors conferences.

Volunteers can work on the helpline, which is based in Norwich, but they can do this work from home. They would be expected to donate three to four hours a week and are given training and support.

Volunteers can also help by organising or participating in fundraising events.

The Encephalitis Society

Website: www.encephalitis.info
Email: support@encephalitis.info
Tel: 01653 699599

The Encephalitis Society works with people who have encephalitis.

It helps both those who have contracted encephalitis and those indirectly affected by it such as carers, family and friends. It also supports research into the condition, provides information, and seeks to raise awareness.

Its services include a telephone helpline that offers support to adults, children and their families. It helps to organise family weekends and retreats; arranges conferences, seminars and retreats for professionals; and maintains a contact scheme for members, who can join the society for free.

Volunteers can help to raise funds and public awareness. The organisation's committee members and trustees are also volunteers.

The Haemophilia Society

Website: www.haemophilia.org.uk
Email: info@haemophilia.org.uk
Tel: 020 7831 1020

The Haemophilia Society, a charity, works with people with haemophilia or other bleeding disorders to secure the best possible care, treatment and support.

Established in 1950, it also helps families, friends and carers of people with bleeding disorders. The organisation has more than 2,000 members and a network of 17 local groups throughout the UK.

Its services provide information, advice, advocacy and support to individuals, including those who have contracted HIV and hepatitis C as a result of treatment with tainted blood. The charity campaigns for improved care and treatment, and it offers grants for research into bleeding disorders, treatment and care.

Volunteers can work in a number of different roles, including assisting at fundraising events.

Leukaemia Research

Website: www.lrf.org.uk
Email: info@lrf.org.uk
Tel: 020 7405 0101

Leukaemia Research, a cancer charity, works to find cures and improve treatments for the 110,000 people in the UK living with leukaemia and related cancers of the blood.

Volunteers can help in a range of ways, either in their local area or by joining the team at its London HQ. The charity, along with its 150 voluntary branches and fundraising groups across the UK, organises many events throughout the year. Support and encouragement is given to all volunteers, whatever level of involvement they choose to have.

Marie Curie Cancer Care

Website: www.mariecurie.org.uk
Tel: 020 7599 7777

Marie Curie Cancer Care is a charity that offers care to about 25,000 people with cancer every year, along with support for their families.

Established in 1948, it employs more than 2,700 nurses, doctors and other healthcare professionals in the UK. The charity also cares for people with other life-limiting illnesses. Services are free of charge to patients and their families.

Its nurses work in the community to provide end-of-life care for patients in their own homes. The charity has ten hospices and two centres for palliative care research. The Marie Curie Research Institute investigates the causes and treatments of cancer.

Around 70% of the charity's income comes from donations from individuals, membership organisations and businesses, with the balance of funds coming from the NHS.

Volunteers can:

- organise or participate in fundraising events
- give their time in one of the charity's shops
- work in one of the offices
- work with a support group
- donate their professional skills, anything from physiotherapy to driving

The Meningitis Trust

Website: www.meningitis-trust.org
Tel: 01453 768000

The Meningitis Trust works to raise awareness of meningitis and septicaemia (blood poisoning) among healthcare professionals and the general public, and to support individuals and families affected by the disease.

The Trust also runs a befriending scheme which allows people who share similar experiences of meningitis to meet and support each other.

Working in their local communities, volunteers help to raise awareness of meningitis to help support the Trust's work. Volunteers also offer support by planning and assisting at fundraising events that take place nationwide. Other volunteers donate their time to help with general administration. Volunteers support the Trust across all areas of its work

The Men's Health Forum

Website: www.menshealthforum.org.uk
Tel: 020 7388 4449

The Men's Health Forum works to improve the health and wellbeing of men in England and Wales.

The forum aims to provide information, raise awareness and stimulate debate about the specific health issues of men. It seeks to encourage men to prioritise their own health and to access medical and other services.

It also campaigns for research, policy and projects that take account of men's health issues and the specific problems they face.

It offers a bookshop, a library and a journal, and organises projects on issues such as men's fitness, prostate cancer, bowel cancer, medications and mental health.

Volunteers can help the Forum in many ways, including assisting with fundraising.

Mind

Website: www.mind.org.uk
Tel: 020 8519 2122

Mind, a charity, campaigns on behalf of those with mental illness in England and Wales.

The charity aims to support and advocate for people with mental health problems, challenge discrimination about mental illness, and influence mental health policy through campaigning and education. It also campaigns for better mental health services.

Mind's services include a helpline, which offers callers confidential help on mental health issues. The charity has a network of more than 200 local associations, which provide supported housing, crisis helplines, drop-in centres, counselling, befriending, advocacy, employment and training schemes, and other services.

It has a network of more than 2,100 users of mental health services, who seek to support each other, share experiences and develop skills.

Mind also campaigns for legal rights for the mentally ill and to change attitudes toward mental health problems among employers. And it advises government, health and local authorities and the public on best practice, services and developments in mental health community care.

Volunteers can help with fundraising, either by participating in structured events or by organising a sponsored local event.

The Miscarriage Association

Website: www.miscarriageassociation.org.uk
Email: info@miscarriageassociation.org.uk
Tel: 01924 200795

The Miscarriage Association, a charity, offers support to parents who have had a miscarriage.

In addition to helping parents, it also supports and provides information to partners, other family, or to friends who have been affected by miscarriage.

The charity has a helpline that provides support by telephone, letter or email. Its network of support volunteers, some of whom have had a miscarriage themselves, offers one-to-one support.

It has local support groups, publishes information, leaflets and fact sheets, and encourages research into the causes, management and prevention of pregnancy loss. In addition, the charity seeks to raise awareness about the issue and to lobby for improved services.

Volunteers can:

- become a telephone support volunteer (some helpline volunteers are bilingual)
- set up or help to run a support group
- become a health liaison volunteer by working with the charity's distance learning pack
- become a member of the trustee board

Positively Women

Website: www.positivelywomen.org.uk
Tel: 020 7713 0222

Positively Women is a charity that works with women affected by HIV and with their families.

The charity aims to improve the life of women with HIV by offering support services, including one-to-one and peer support, family work, a drugs and prison scheme, an immigration project and complementary therapies.

Every year, it works with more than 1,000 women with HIV. All of its services are free.

Volunteers can help in a range of ways including fundraising, or by serving on the management committee. Volunteers are trained.

The Prostate Cancer Charity

Website: www.prostate-cancer.org.uk
Email: info@prostate-cancer.org.uk
Tel: 020 8222 7622

The Prostate Cancer Charity offers support and information to anyone concerned about prostate cancer.

Established in 1996, it operates a free helpline. It organises events and projects and seeks to raise public awareness about the disease. It has also invested nearly £5 million in medical research into prostate cancer and its treatment.

The charity's projects include Prostate Cancer Awareness Week, an annual campaign. It also runs a project to raise awareness about the likelihood of Afro-Caribbean men contracting prostate cancer.

In addition, it has a programme that seeks to place nurses who are specially trained in prostate cancer treatment in the NHS with the goal of improving practice at the local level.

Volunteers can help by organising fundraising events.

React

Website: www.reactcharity.org
Email: react@reactcharity.org
Tel: 020 8940 2575

React, a charity, works with children with life-limiting illnesses.

The charity, also known as Rapid Effective Assistance for Children with Potentially Terminal illness, helps severely ill children from low-income households. It aims to provide the help quickly and with a minimum of red tape.

Its services include supplying equipment, ranging from specialist wheelchairs, beds, baths and mobility aids to everyday items like washing machines and tumble dryers.

React also offers financial support, for example to enable a family to travel to hospital. It works with children's hospices and other support services, and with medical professionals involved in paediatric care.

It funds research and education projects aimed at improving the quality of life for severely ill children. In addition, it offers family holidays in one of its five holiday homes.

Volunteers can help in many different ways, for example:

- helping in the office in Kew, in Surrey
- copywriting
- PR and marketing
- Helping at a fundraising event
- working directly with families

Refuge

Website: www.refuge.org.uk
Email: volunteering@refuge.org.uk
Tel: 020 7395 7700

Refuge, a charity, provides emergency accommodation and support to women and children who are affected by domestic violence.

Refuge aims to provide safe refuges and services for women and children who are experiencing physical, sexual, emotional or financial abuse. The charity also aims to raise awareness about domestic violence and to eliminate it.

It provides individual and group counselling for children, individuals and groups. It offers community-based outreach for women, including outreach that is geared towards members of ethnic minority communities.

The charity runs a free 24-hour helpline, run in partnership with the charity Women's Aid. The helpline offers support, information and help with accessing women's refuges.

The support and information given by Refuge is also available for friends, family members and external agencies calling on behalf of a woman or child. Men experiencing domestic violence can get referrals to agencies that cater specifically for men.

Volunteers can:

- work on specific fundraising projects during office hours
- help with events, appeals, research and design
- female volunteers can work on the helpline, where training is provided

Relate

Website: www.relate.org.uk
Email: enquiries@relate.org.uk
Tel: 0845 456 1310

Relate, a charity, provides counselling, sex therapy and other support services for those in relationships.

The charity seeks to help couples, families and individuals through all stages of their relationships. Relate counsellors also work with parents and young people and with businesses.

Support can be accessed face-to-face, singly or with others, or via telephone or internet. The charity offers services at more than 600 locations, including community buildings, schools and workplaces.

Volunteers can donate time as a member of the board of trustees. Each of the charity's centres is governed by a board of trustees, who are also voting members of the charity's governing body.

Other opportunities for volunteering include:

- working in a charity shop
- working as a receptionist or administrator
- offering expert support at a centre
- working in information technology

Release

Website: www.release.org.uk
Email: ask@release.org.uk
Tel: 020 7729 5255

Release is a charity that provides advice and information on drugs, the law and human rights.

Founded in 1967, its services were originally aimed at drug users, their families and friends. The charity's services are now also offered to professionals from statutory and voluntary agencies.

Through its legal services programme, a team of lawyers backed by administrative support staff and volunteers offers advice and information on drugs and the law through a legal helpline. The charity also runs weekly outreach programmes in London.

These free services are available to anyone who is directly or indirectly affected by drugs and the law. Release also provides support for professionals seeking to stay abreast of legislation on drugs, and for members of the public who are concerned about a drug-related problem.

Release's drug services, such as the heroin helpline, offer specialist advice on drugs.

Opportunities for volunteers include working on telephone helplines. Training is provided.

The Royal British Legion

Website: www.poppy.org.uk and www.britishlegion.org.uk
Email: poppypeople@britishlegion.org.uk
Tel: 0800 085 5924

The Royal British Legion, a charity, helps people who have served or are serving in the British armed forces.

Its work helps people financially, socially and emotionally. Nearly 10.5 million people are eligible for its assistance, including dependants of servicemen and women.

The charity has welfare caseworkers who provide emotional support and practical assistance for ex-servicemen and women, including visiting those who are housebound or in hospital, and giving advice on pensions and residential or nursing care.

It runs the annual Poppy Appeal during November, which raises almost one-third of the Legion's annual welfare budget of £75 million. It is also the nation's custodian of Remembrance.

Volunteers can:

- work as 'poppy people', collecting donations on the streets
- help to plan the poppy collections
- work as caseworkers in the community

Samaritans

Website: www.samaritans.org
Email: admin@samaritans.org
Tel: 020 8394 8300

Samaritans, a charity, provides confidential, emotional support to people experiencing distress or despair or contemplating suicide.

Established in 1953, it aims to give people an opportunity to talk or seek further help by telephone or via email, text message or mail. Although Samaritans has its origin in the church, it is not a religious organisation.

Samaritans now has 202 branches across the UK and Ireland, and about 17,000 volunteers who staff phonelines round the clock. In 2005, some 5 million people used the charity's support services.

Volunteers can work on the phoneline or by answering emails or other communication. Training is provided. Most volunteers work for a few hours weekly.

SANELINE

Website: www.sane.org.uk
Email: volunteer@sane.org.uk
Tel: 020 7422 5535

SANELINE offers out-of-hours help for anyone affected by a mental health problem.

The organisation aims to offer callers emotional support and information, and, if appropriate, to encourage them to benefit from the network of care in their own area. The range of information includes mental illness, options for more help, treatments and therapies, law, self-harm and suicide.

Callers can include carers, family, friends and health professionals in addition to those experiencing mental health problems themselves. The phone line, operated by the mental health charity SANE, is offered in more than 100 different languages and for the hard of hearing. It is open from 1 p.m. to 11 p.m. daily.

Volunteers can work on the helpline. They are required to take a training course, which is approved by the Royal College of Psychiatrists. The course is also accredited by the National Open College Network. No previous experience is necessary. Ongoing training is also provided.

Volunteers, once trained, are expected to stay for at least one year, filling a weekly four-hour shift. Volunteers can commit to whatever time slot suits them.

Sue Ryder Care

Website: www.suerydercare.org
Tel: 020 7400 0440

Sue Ryder Care, a charity, helps people with neurological diseases and life-limiting illnesses both in the UK and overseas.

The charity also helps the families, carers and friends of people with life-limiting illnesses. Its services include long-term and respite residential care, day care and home care.

Volunteers can help in all areas of the organisation's work, from providing support and company to people in its care to working in an administrative role or supporting staff in the charity shops. In addition, volunteers help to raise funds and public awareness of the charity.

Terrence Higgins Trust

Website: www.tht.org.uk
Email: info@tht.org.uk
Tel: 020 7812 1600

Terrence Higgins Trust is a charity that provides information and services related to HIV and sexual health in England, Wales and Scotland.

The largest HIV and sexual health charity in the UK, it provides services including THT Direct, a helpline that offers emotional support and information on how to access services including counselling, HIV testing, treatment advice, information about benefits, employment, immigration, housing and legal advice.

The charity also aims to help individuals to access support groups, grants and complementary therapies. It provides education for the community about HIV and sexually transmitted diseases, and it campaigns and lobbies to raise awareness about the impacts of HIV and sexual health.

In addition the charity has a new service in London for refugees and asylum seekers.

Volunteers can help the charity by:

- volunteering on the helpline (full training is provided)
- supporting clients in their home
- covering the reception and switchboard of each centre
- offering administrative support

TimeBank

Back to Life

Website: www.backtolife.org.uk

Tel: 0845 601 4008

Back to Life is a London-based mentoring scheme that offers practical and emotional support for young men who are recovering from mental health issues.

Male volunteer mentors are matched with men of a similar age who have had mental health problem and are looking to get back into employment or education. As a team, the mentor and mentee set goals and plan how to achieve them in small steps. Trained mentors offer impartial advice aiming to provide mentees with the support they need to get on with their life.

Volunteers spend about five hours a month with their mentee. Both mentors and mentees are given full training before meeting.

HOUSING AND HOMELESSNESS

Bield Housing Association

Website: www.bield.co.uk
Email: info@bield.co.uk
Tel: 0131 273 4000

Bield Housing Association provides housing, care and support services for older people in Scotland.

Its aim is to allow older people to live independently. The Association provides housing - some of it sheltered - and services such as respite care and day care to approximately 15,000 older people. Its community alarm system offers emergency response to 29,000 households in housing associations and local authorities across Scotland.

Volunteers must be aged 16 or over. They can:

- help to organise social activities such as tea and coffee sessions, lunch clubs, outings, games and crafts, or reminiscence groups
- become a befriender, visiting tenants who are isolated, accompanying them on outings or giving extra support on a regular basis

Broadway

Website: www.broadwaylondon.org
Email: broadway@broadwaylondon.org
Tel: 020 7089 950

Broadway helps single people in London who face homelessness or who are homeless.

The organisation's aim is to ensure that homeless people find and retain a home. Created in 2002 from the merger of Riverpoint and Housing Services Agency, it helps approximately 2,800 people.

It provides a range of services, from hostels to funding for basic household items. It gives help with welfare, alternative healthcare and peer education. Broadway also works with and encourages other agencies that support homeless people, and tries to raise public awareness.

Volunteer opportunities include:

- befriending
- organising and facilitating activities
- interpreting
- administration
- research
- helping in hostels, resource rooms and day centres

Crisis

Website: www.crisis.org.uk
Email: volunteering@crisis.org.uk
Tel: 0870 011 3335

Crisis is a charity that works with single homeless people.

Its primary aim is to work with homeless people who are not on the streets but living in places such as hostels and bed and breakfasts, or sleeping on friends' and family's floors.

The charity offers services, some in partnership with other organisations, to help single homeless people to overcome addictions or mental health problems. It commissions and publishes research, campaigns and organises events to raise awareness. Over Christmas, it runs seven centres in London, offering companionship, meals and other services.

Volunteers can help by:

- working directly with homeless people
- providing administrative support
- raising funds
- helping with educational programmes
- raising awareness about the charity's work
- working on campaigns
- helping with the logistics of the charity's operations, by driving vehicles, coordinating food deliveries, and translating

W welcoming guests and serving food at the Christmas events, washing hair or sorting bedding

Emmaus

Website: www.emmaus.org.uk
Email: contact@emmaus.org.uk
Tel: 01223 379271

Emmaus operates Communities where formerly homeless men and women can live and work with support.

Emmaus, founded by a Catholic priest in Paris in 1949, is a non-religious group that runs more than 400 Communities in the UK and worldwide. There are 13 in the UK. Its goal is to make the Communities become self-sufficient.

The residents work full time, collecting, refurbishing and reselling furniture at on-site shops. In return, they receive accommodation, food, clothing and a weekly allowance.

If the Community makes a surplus, it is used to establish new Emmaus Communities, or given away to help projects for others in need, such as local shelters and soup kitchens for the homeless, helping victims of the tsunami in 2004 and building a village primary school in Swaziland.

The Communities are usually located in refurbished buildings, including abandoned factories, schools and convents. There are Emmaus Communities in Bristol, Cambridge, Brighton, Dover, Greenwich, Bolton, St Albans, Carlton in Bedfordshire, Gloucester, Mossley in Greater Manchester, Leeds, Glasgow and Coventry. Six more Communities are due to open over the next few years.

Emmaus is also building its first green building in the UK - Emmaus Hampshire, expected to open in 2008 - using sustainable materials and techniques.

Volunteers can work in roles such as:

- trustee members
- shop attendants
- van drivers
- fundraisers

Positions are available at all Communities, established and new, and at the central office in Cambridge.

The National Housing Federation

Website: www.housing.org.uk/getonboard
Email: corinem@housing.org.uk
Tel: 020 7067 1034

The National Housing Federation supports housing associations throughout England and campaigns for better neighbourhoods and more affordable housing.

It represents and supports 1,400 associations that provide two million homes for five million people. The residents part-own or rent their accommodation at below market rates. The housing associations are independent and not-for-profit organisations.

The member associations are usually involved in housing regeneration and in work that aims to strengthen the local community. They vary greatly in size from national providers with tens of thousands of homes to small local charities. Some of the associations also offer specialist services such as support for the homeless or care homes for older people.

Volunteers can join the board of a housing association, working on issues such as the strategic direction of the association, access to housing and community safety. The National Housing Federation's Get On Board scheme matches volunteers with housing associations that need board members.

Training for board membership is provided, as are out-of-pocket expenses or childcare costs so that volunteers can attend board meetings. The time commitment is usually the equivalent of one day a month.

Nomad

Website: www.nomadsheffield.co.uk
Email: volunteers@nomadsheffield.co.uk
Tel: 0114 263 6624

Nomad Homeless Advice and Support Unit works with the homeless and with people who are inadequately housed in Sheffield and Rotherham.

Founded by two people who were once homeless themselves, it aims to ensure that people can live in safe, affordable homes. It offers information, re-housing and help with benefits claims and debt.

Schemes include an advice centre in central Sheffield, help for tenants who are at risk of becoming homeless, and a project that supports young people aged 16 to 25 who either have, or will soon have, their own home.

The organisation offers a bond guarantee scheme to help the homeless gain access to the rental market. Its residential project in Rotherham provides beds for young homeless people aged 16 to 25.

Volunteers work with all of the services that Nomad offers. Opportunities include:

- administration
- offering advice
- reception work
- inputting data
- tenancy support
- befriending
- mentoring
- helping at a young persons' drop-in centre
- serving on the organisation's management committee

Shelter

Website: www.shelter.org.uk
Email: info@shelter.org.uk
Tel: 0845 458 4590

Shelter is a charity that works on housing issues and with the homeless.

It aims to help homeless people to find and keep an affordable home and to ensure that enough housing is available. Every year, the charity helps 170,000 people with housing needs

Shelter also campaigns for new laws and policies that help the homeless to gain access to housing, and produces publications that offer information on housing issues.

The charity conducts research into housing, and it trains individuals and agencies in the housing sector.

Volunteers can:

- work in charity shops

- help at fundraising events
- campaign at a regional or national level
- assist with a specific project
- befriend newly housed people and help them to obtain services
- help with decorating or gardening

St Matthew Housing

Website: www.stmatthewhousing.org
Email: info@stmatthewhousing.org
Tel: 01284 732550

St Matthew Housing works with homeless people in East Anglia and the East Midlands.

The organisation provides housing for more than 600 people and community support to hundreds more. Its central office is in Bury St Edmunds.

It has three types of accommodation: supported housing, group homes, and flats for those who are closer to finding their own home.

In the houses, the organisation offers day-to-day support. In group homes, residents shop and cook for themselves, although staff are nearby should help be needed. The flats allow residents to live independently, although they can still access help if required. St Matthew Housing also has a programme that supports residents who are not in the organisation's own accommodation.

Volunteering opportunities include:

- working in group houses
- befriending and supporting residents
- acting as an advocate
- assisting with fundraising and street collections
- selling the organisation's Christmas cards

OLDER PEOPLE

The Abbeyfield Society

Website: www.abbeyfield.com
Email: post@abbeyfield.com
Tel: 01727 857536

The Abbeyfield Society, a volunteer-led charity, provides housing, support and companionship to older people in their own communities. Its aim is to make older people's lives easier and more fulfilling.

The charity provides 800 sheltered houses, with support for the residents and two meals per day, across the UK.

It also has about 80 residential homes that have 24-hour personal care for those who are frail. In addition, Abbeyfield offers day care and is developing services for people with dementia.

Volunteers can work as local trustees of a society, becoming a member of a house committee that manages the house and its staff. They can help in other ways too - by befriending the residents, talking to them, taking them shopping, transporting them to visit doctors and other medical services, organising social outings and birthdays, and flower arranging.

Action on Elder Abuse

Website: www.elderabuse.org.uk
Email: enquiries@elderabuse.org.uk
Tel: 020 8769 7000

Action on Elder Abuse (AEA) works to protect and prevent the abuse of vulnerable older people in the UK and Ireland.

Based in London, the charity was established by a group of practitioners from health and social care, academia and the voluntary sector who were concerned about the lack of assistance for those who were abused or at risk of abuse.

The charity runs a helpline that offers information, advice and support to victims and others who are concerned about or have witnessed abuse.

AEA also aims to raise awareness by encouraging education, promoting research, and collecting and disseminating information. It runs conferences on elder abuse and related issues; produces leaflets, resource materials and reports for practitioners and the public; and acts as a resource for television, radio and the press.

Volunteers can work in fundraising.

Age Concern

Website: www.ageconcern.org.uk
Tel: 020 8765 7200

Age Concern offers support to all people over 50 years old in the UK.

The organisation aims to ensure they get the most from life, by providing services and information. It campaigns on issues including age discrimination and pensions, and works to influence public opinion and government policy.

Most of Age Concern's work is carried out locally, through advocacy and advice services, day care, lunch clubs, home and after-hospital help, 'handyperson' schemes, leisure activities, and training on issues such as IT, health or nutrition.

In some local areas, the organisation also provides befriending and home visiting services, counselling, exercise classes, foot care and mobility aids.

Volunteers are able to help with all of the services offered. Local Age Concern shops may also require volunteer helpers.

Contact the Elderly

Website: www.contact-the-elderly.org
Email: info@contact-the-elderly.org.uk
Tel: 0800 716543

Contact the Elderly is a small national charity that seeks to reduce the isolation and loneliness of very elderly people who live alone.

The charity holds Sunday afternoon tea parties once a month for small groups of people aged 75 and older who have little contact with family or friends. The tea party is hosted by a different volunteer each month. Transport is provided.

More than 300 parties are held across the UK, each catering for about six to eight older people. The tea parties each require three to four drivers and up to twelve hosts, all of whom are volunteers.

Volunteers can work either as drivers or hosts. As drivers, they must be able to commit to a few hours each month. Hosts must have a downstairs sitting room and toilet and easy access into the house or garden.

Help the Aged

Website: www.helptheaged.org.uk
Email: info@helptheaged.org.uk
Tel: 020 7278 1114

Help the Aged is an international charity working to reduce poverty, isolation and neglect amongst older people.

In the UK, the charity offers advice and information on topics such as finance, health, housing and care. It offers the help through phonelines, face-to-face projects, booklets and other publications.

The charity also campaigns for change in government policy, undertakes research into the needs of older people and delivers social services across the UK and overseas.

Overseas, it supports HIV and Aids treatment programmes for older people and offers general health schemes, emergency relief and financial sponsorship.

The charity has diverse opportunities for volunteers in the UK. Volunteers can befriend or visit an older person, or work in a Help the Aged shop, a branch office or at a fundraising event.

TimeBank
Time of Your Life

Website: www.timelife.org.uk
Email: info@backtolife.org.uk
Tel: 0845 601 4008

Time of Your Life is a scheme based in the London Borough of Brent that gives older people who are feeling the effects of isolation (Friends) the opportunity to be matched with volunteers (Befrienders). Friends and Befrienders are of a similar age and a different ethnic background.

Befrienders offer companionship, visiting their Friends on a regular basis, as well as taking them on outings when possible. They are also encouraged to attend regular social events together.

Time of Your Life aims to celebrate the diversity found in Brent, a borough rich in many cultures, with 120 languages spoken. However, Brent also suffers from segregation, with older people from different ethnic communities mainly living and socialising within their own communities.

YOUTH AND YOUNG PEOPLE

Changemakers

Website: www.changemakers.org.uk
Email: info@changemakers.org
Tel: 020 7702 1511

Changemakers has an overall aim to motivate young people to become more active members of society by providing a platform for them to get actively involved in their local communities.

It also hopes to prepare them for the working world by encouraging them to be independent, use their initiative, think creatively about problem-solving, develop strategy skills and see projects through to completion.

Changemakers supports youth volunteering in a number of ways. It delivers a range of learning programmes to schools, youth organisations, community groups and employers. The bespoke products and services it provides to organisations enable these groups to develop their thinking and practice in enterprise, citizenship, youth participation and leadership.

Changemakers also offers funding to innovative schemes and undertakes research. It advocates the youth-led approach to policymakers and practitioners. For example, the Russell Commission addresses inconsistencies and weaknesses in provision, which prevent the full potential of youth volunteering opportunities from being realised, as well as identifying ways to engage more young people from disadvantaged and under-represented communities.

The Duke of Edinburgh's Award

Website: www.theaward.org
Tel: 01753 727400

The Duke of Edinburgh's Award is a programme for the personal development of young people

The Award is made up of components including

- service (helping people in the community)
- skills (including hobbies and interests)
- physical recreation (sport, dance and fitness)
- expeditions (training for, planning and completing a journey on foot or horseback, by boat or cycle)

The Award is widely recognised by employers and people involved in education. Some of the benefits to young people include developing self-confidence and self-reliance, gaining a sense of achievement and a sense of responsibility; discovering new skills, interests and talents and developing leadership skills and abilities. They can also make new friends, experience teamwork, problem-solving and decision-making, increase their motivation, enhance their self-esteem and develop their communication skills.

Volunteering could include:

- helping out at a local Award Group
- being a group leader
- teaching expedition skills
- instructing in a certain sport or skill

Many volunteers share their skills and local knowledge of expeditioning areas in the UK and help to assess visiting groups of Award Participants who are undertaking their expeditions.

Enterprise Education Trust

Website: www.enterprise-education.org.uk
Email: info@enterprise-education.org.uk
Tel: 020 7620 0735

The Enterprise Education Trust aims to empower young people through business and enterprise.

Volunteers from business act as role models on its business awareness and key skills programmes. These volunteers run interactive workshops where they talk about their role in their company and run an exercise based on their area of expertise.

These programmes give students an insight into the world of business, help them to identify and develop their key employability skills, and open their eyes to exciting career opportunities, preparing them for the world of work.

There are benefits for the volunteer too. Many businesses encourage their staff to take part in these programmes because they are an ideal way to develop their own presentation, communication, planning and organisational skills, as part of their continuing professional development.

Envision

Website: www.envision.org.uk
Email: vision@envision.org.uk
Tel: 020 7974 8440

Envision enables sixth-form students aged 16 to 19 to engage with social and environmental issues in their schools and local communities by supporting them in developing their own social and environmental projects.

Envision's aim is to make volunteering appealing to those who would not normally get involved and to challenge attitudes that suggest young people are apathetic and unconcerned with the challenges that face Britain and the world in the 21st century.

Following a presentation given by Envision at the beginning of the school year, interested students form teams of 10–15 members to work on projects on issues of importance to them. EYEs (or Envision Youth Educators) are the volunteers who support a team in implementing a project in their schools or local communities. The role involves providing advice and encouragement at weekly meetings.

EYEs receive training in working with young people and facilitation skills. Envision provides advice, resources and contacts from the central Envision team. It organises networking events to help EYEs learn from each other. All agreed expenses are covered.

Girlguiding UK

Website: www.girlguiding.org.uk
Email: chq@girlguiding.org.uk
Tel: 020 7834 6242

Girlguiding UK is the largest voluntary organisation for girls and young women in the UK, with over 600,000 members. It provides a safe, female-only space for girls and young women to get involved in a wide range of activities, from abseiling and canoeing to circus performance and fashion. Guiding also provides opportunities for international travel, volunteering in the community and camping.

Girlguiding UK needs 8,000 adult volunteers to enable more than 50,000 girls on the waiting list to become members. Volunteers can choose to help Rainbow, Brownie and Guide units as unit helpers, or even take responsibility for running units as a leader. Female volunteers aged 18 to 65 can become leaders after undergoing training and attending specialist sessions. Initially they gain the Girlguiding UK Leadership Qualification and there are further training opportunities available once qualified.

Volunteers do not have to make a regular long-term commitment to guiding. Girlguiding UK offers a range of flexible volunteering roles for busy people, from driving minibuses, to doing accounts, to running PR campaigns. Girlguiding UK also encourages businesses to implement Employee Supported Volunteering (ESV) schemes.

Inter Cultural Youth Exchange

Website: www.icye.org.uk
Email: info@icye.org.uk
Tel: 0870 7743 3486 or 020 7681 0983

Inter Cultural Youth Exchange (ICYE) is a volunteering organisation that aims to promote inter-cultural understanding and international cooperation through the exchange of people and ideas.

ICYE's long-term programmes are for six months or one year and offer the opportunity for candidates to volunteer on one or more projects in their chosen country. ICYE is active in Africa, Latin America, Asia and Europe. Voluntary placements are sourced sensitively by professionals who live and work in the communities in which volunteers are placed.

Volunteers live either with a host family or on the project site. Examples of placements include:

- working with street children
- drug rehabilitation programmes
- promoting HIV/Aids awareness
- general health
- NGO support
- women's rights
- disability support
- teaching
- community development
- human rights

The age range for long-term programmes is 18 to 30, although there is some flexibility in the upper age limit.

Outward Bound

www.outwardbound.org.uk/Trust/Supporters/Associations
enquiries@outwardbound.org.uk
0870 513 4227

Outward Bound® is a non-profit-making educational charity, working to help young people to realise their potential through supportive and challenging outdoor adventures.

It aims to help them to overcome their fears, raise their self-esteem and prepare them to face whatever life throws at them.

Outward Bound® offers a different learning environment from the classroom, with opportunities such as expeditioning, raft building or abseiling.

Participants complete their Outward Bound® adventure as part of a residential course at one of the Trust's centres in UK locations – Ullswater in the English Lake District, Loch Eil near Scotland's Fort William, and Aberdovey on the Welsh coast.

Although volunteer work at the activity centres is not possible, there are other ways to help the Outward Bound Trust. One such way is fundraising. All funds are invested in the organisation, providing more courses for young people who would otherwise not have the opportunity to attend.

The Scout Association

Website: www.scouts.org.uk
Email: info.centre@scout.org.uk
Tel: 0845 300 1818

The Scout Association provides adventurous activities and personal development opportunities for young people from six to 25 years old.

Weekly activities include abseiling, canoeing, archery, caving, climbing and karting.

Scouting aims to encourage development in young people through 'learning by doing'. Scouts are given responsibility, encouraged to work in teams, to take acceptable risks and to think for themselves.

Every section (Beavers, Cubs, Scouts, Explorers and Network) has a leader. The leader has overall responsibility for the running of the section. This means planning and delivering the balanced programme with the help of assistant leaders and section assistants. All leaders are volunteers. They are given training on the job and learn new skills as they go along.

Assistant leaders provide general support such as making refreshments, keeping records up to date and organising games.

Volunteers may take on short-term assignments as well. For example, a qualified first aider could run a one-off interactive session, or someone with an interest in nature could take a group on a walk through the local woods.

Sea Cadets

Website: www.sea-cadets.org
Email: info@ms-sc.org
Tel: 020 7654 7000

The Sea Cadets is a nationwide voluntary youth organisation that runs activities including sailing and canoeing, abseiling, engineering, music and cookery.

The Sea Cadets is open to young people aged 12 to 18, and the junior section is open to children aged 10 to 12. There are 386 units in communities across the UK.

It has a structure modelled on that of the Royal Navy, giving Cadets an opportunity to progress and take up positions of responsibility as they acquire skills. On reaching 18, many Cadets choose to stay on as adult instructors, when their training and talents can be used to support younger Cadets.

Units are run by adult volunteers who are needed not only to instruct the Cadets, but also to provide assistance. This help ranges from driving the minibus or making packed lunches, to negotiating with the local council or organising the record keeping, re-painting the facilities or fundraising.

TheSite.org

Website: www.thesite.org
Email: feedback@thesite.org
Tel: 020 7226 8008

TheSite.org aims to be the first place young adults between the ages of 16 and 24 turn to when they need support and guidance through life.

It aims to provide online access to high-quality, impartial information and advice to support young people in making their own decisions.

TheSite.org provides fact sheets and articles on key issues facing young people including sex and relationships, drinking and drugs, work and study, housing, the law, finances and health and wellbeing.

Users can seek peer-to-peer support and advise each other on the issues concerning them.

Volunteers are needed to act as online peer advisers and moderators. Peer advisers support young people by answering their questions on relationships. Moderators check posts made by bulletin-board users. Most of the time no action needs to be taken, but occasionally someone needs help (for instance, someone with depression may need reassurance and a helpline number), or posters need to be warned about unacceptable behaviour (for instance commercial advertising or racist remarks). Repeat offenders have their posts removed and sometimes have to be banned. Moderators help to keep the atmosphere positive and friendly.

TimeBank
Young TimeBank

Website: www.youngtimebank.org.uk
Tel: 020 7785 6374

Young TimeBank encourages young people to take control of the issues they feel strongly about by developing and managing their own community projects. Volunteers lend a hand along the way, empowering young people to make their big ideas happen.

Examples of Young TimeBank's projects are youth centres, radio stations, anti-vandalism events, anti-racism campaigns, putting on concerts and exhibitions and making short films.

YMCA

Website: www.ymca.org.uk
Email: enquiries@ymca.org.uk
Tel: 0845 873 6633

The YMCA provides services that are relevant to young people, particularly those who are vulnerable, disadvantaged, or hard to reach.

Every YMCA in England is locally and independently managed and works to meet the specific needs of young people in their local communities.

From providing housing, training and community health and fitness facilities to helping young people and their families, YMCAs in over 250 communities in England encourage, support and challenge young people. For example, they offer a range of services designed to increase the employability and financial awareness of young people, helping them to find and keep jobs. They hope to empower young people by involving them in activities that stimulate, challenge and enable them to realise their potential and participate fully in their communities.

The YMCA delivers a range of other services in such areas as health and physical activity, crime prevention, parenting and family, and it provides safe, supported accommodation for single men and women between the ages of 16 and 35.

Volunteering opportunities are available at a local level, via individual YMCAs. These are wide-ranging and can include:

- opportunities in youth work
- fitness instruction
- administration
- providing short-term emergency accommodation for homeless young people
- working in a YMCA shop
- sitting on the board of a local YMCA

Youth Action Network

Website: www.youth-action.org.uk
Email: info@youth-action.org.uk
Tel: 0121 455 9732

Youth Action Network is a national membership organisation that creates opportunities for young people to participate in volunteering and develop their own solutions to community needs.

It works towards this by supporting the development of diverse, progressive and sustainable organisations, by promoting youth participation more widely and by encouraging organisations that engage young people.

Youth Action Network believes that young people's own interests and motivations will drive their volunteering experience and that recruitment is much more successful when young people are involved in the enrolment of their peers.

Because of the element of youth control, youth action projects encourage progression into community activism from democratic activism such as UK Youth Parliament or local youth or school councils.

Youth Action Network encourages young people to put their time and energy into providing services, producing resources, creating new ideas and generally making positive contributions to their community groups, the environment and their own lives.

Youth at Risk UK

Website: www.youthatrisk.org.uk
Email: susan@youthatrisk.org.uk
Tel: 01763 241120

Youth at Risk designs, develops and delivers social intervention programmes aimed at enabling alienated young people to transform the way they view and live their lives.

Many of these people have demonstrated aggressive antisocial behaviour, committed crime, abused drugs and alcohol, truanted from school or are unemployed.

Youth at Risk works to encourage and coach them to reinvent themselves and choose to live responsibly.

An example of the type of project that Youth at Risk runs was chronicled in the Channel 4 series Ballet Changed My Life: Ballet Hoo!. This project combined personal development and life skills coaching with a demanding regime of ballet training to bring about a transformation to the lives of a group of young people from Birmingham and the Black Country.

Youth at Risk's professional trainers are supported by volunteers who are given rigorous training to enable them to give life coaching to alienated young people. After volunteers are matched one-to-one with programme participants, they maintain contact with them at least once a week, supporting them throughout the duration of the project.

UMBRELLA ORGANISATIONS

CSV

Website: www.csv.org.uk
Email: information@csv.org.uk
Tel: 020 7278 6601

CSV is a nationwide volunteering charity which provides volunteers with information, advice, support and development services. CSV matches volunteers to organisations, helps to develop or run volunteering programmes, organises employee volunteering schemes, and provides professional development for employees who volunteer. It offers media training for both individuals and voluntary sector organisations, covering radio, video, TV, print, web and other new media. Training ranges from courses in basic skills to complex multi-media training. Its various campaigns include Make a Difference Day and Action Earth.

Do-it

Website: www.do-it.org.uk
Tel: 020 7226 8008

do-it.org.uk is volunteering made easy. Launched in 2001 by the online charity Youthnet, do-it.org.uk is the most diverse and comprehensive national database of volunteering opportunities in the UK. Its quick and simple postcode search scans hundreds of thousands of opportunities to volunteer, providing an instant list of volunteering acitivities in your area. Most of the opportunities on do-it.org.uk come from local Volunteer Centres in England and national charities. And each month, do-it.org.uk attracts an average of 50,000 visitors.

The Media Trust

Website: www.mediatrust.org
Email: info@mediatrust.org
Tel: 020 7874 7600

The Media Trust seeks to help charities to communicate by giving media training and running communications seminars and workshops. It also provides resources, information and contacts. The Media Trust runs a media matching service whereby organisations can register for help from media and communications professionals.

National Association for Voluntary and Community Action

Website: www.navca.org.uk
Email: navca@navca.org.uk
Tel: 0114 278 6636

The National Association for Voluntary and Community Action (NAVCA) is a body supporting the local voluntary and community sector infrastructure in England. It has 360 members working in 140,000 local community groups and voluntary organisations to provide services for their communities. It provides members with information, advice, networking and learning opportunities, support and development services. In partnership with local public bodies, NAVCA members work to regenerate neighbourhoods, increase volunteering and tackle discrimination.

NAVCA draws on the experiences of its members to influence government and contribute to national policy. It also works closely with other national bodies to ensure a collaborative approach to policy development.

National Association for Voluntary Service Managers

Website: navsm.volunteering.org.uk

The National Association for Voluntary Service Managers (NAVSM) is concerned with managers in the fields of health and social care.

NAVSM aims to advise employers on the role, duties, recruitment and training of a voluntary service manager, to promote suitable training and adequate qualifications for members and to provide opportunities for mutual support. It also aims to represent the interest of members where statutory and other bodies are concerned and to publicise the work of the voluntary service manager.

The National Council for Voluntary Organisations

Website: www.ncvo-vol.org.uk
Email: ncvo@ncvo-vol.org.uk
Tel: 020 7713 6161

The National Council for Voluntary Organisations (NCVO) is the umbrella body for the voluntary sector in England. Its services include a freephone HelpDesk, policy briefings, information networks, events and a wide range of publications.

Northern Ireland Council for Voluntary Action

Website: www.nicva.org
Email: info@nicva.org
Tel: 028 9087 7777

The Northern Ireland Council for Voluntary Action (NICVA) is the umbrella body for voluntary and community organisations in Northern Ireland. Its mission is to achieve progressive social change by tackling disadvantage through voluntary action and community development. Its services include information, advice, membership support, policy and research.

Northern Ireland Volunteering Development Agency

Website: www.volunteering-ni.org
Email: info@volunteering-ni.org
Tel: 028 9023 610

Northern Ireland Volunteering Development Agency (NIVDA) aims to promote volunteering and improve the quality of the involvement of volunteers in Northern Ireland. The Agency provides a central resource of support, information and training to those who work with volunteers across all sectors.

Scottish Council for Voluntary Organisations

Website: www.scvo.org.uk
Email: enquiries@scvo.org.uk
Tel: 0131 556 3882

The Scottish Council for Voluntary Organisations (SCVO) is the umbrella body for voluntary organisations in Scotland. SCVO seeks to advance the values and interests shared by voluntary organisations by fostering cooperation and promoting best practice, and by the delivery of sustainable common services.

Its services include: information, research, campaigning, conferences and seminars, training, recruitment and workforce development, advice, publications, ICT support, computer software, office supplies, a payroll bureau, pensions, bespoke insurance policies, project development and management, Charity Giving Scotland and Give As You Earn, and direct links with Councils for Voluntary Service and national networks.

TimeBank

Website: www.timebank.org.uk
Tel: 0845 456 1668

TimeBank is a national charity that provides people with the inspiration, opportunities and support to volunteer. TimeBank was created for people who know their time and skills are in demand, but do not know where to begin.

TimeBank constantly develops new, exciting ways to involve volunteers and its projects address very real needs. If none of TimeBank's own projects suit your current situation, it can also match you with thousands of volunteering opportunities right across the country through its relationship with a network across the country.

People who register with TimeBank have access to an online chat forum where they can get all their volunteering questions answered. They also receive a regular newsletter with the latest volunteering ideas, advice and news.

Volunteer Development Scotland

Website: www.vds.org.uk
Email: vds@vds.org.uk
Tel: 01786 479593

Volunteer Development Scotland works strategically and in partnership to help to create an enabling environment for volunteering in Scotland. Its services include information, advice, membership support, training, a learning centre, policy and research.

Volunteering England

Website: www.volunteering.org.uk
Email: volunteering@volunteeringengland.org
Tel: 0845 305 6979

Volunteering England is a national volunteer development organisation for England. It works across the voluntary, public and private sectors to raise the profile of volunteering as a force for change.

Key activities undertaken by Volunteering England include:

- working to secure and support an England-wide network of quality volunteer development agencies, promoting and enabling volunteering and community involvement
- undertaking research, policy and development activity
- providing grants, support and advice to sustain and develop volunteering
- keeping volunteering high on the policy agenda, working with government to promote opportunities for, and remove institutional barriers to, volunteering
- providing authoritative, up-to-date research on volunteering issues
- supporting volunteering development through:
    - promoting accredited quality frameworks for volunteering management and local volunteer development agencies
    - convening national events and practitioner networks
    - mounting awareness campaigns
    - providing consultancy, education, training, publications, information and web-based services
    - providing grants and strategic support to the work of volunteers
    - identifying, disseminating and promoting good practice in the involvement of volunteers

Wales Council for Voluntary Action

Website: www.wcva.org.uk
Email: help@wcva.org.uk
Tel: 0870 607 1666

The Wales Council for Voluntary Action (WCVA) is the umbrella body for voluntary and community organisations in Wales. WCVA offers information, funding services, publications about the voluntary sector, a library and membership services for voluntary organisations.

Worldwide Volunteering

Website: www.worldwidevolunteering.org.uk
Email: wwv@wwv.org.uk
Tel: 01935 825588

The aim of WorldWide Volunteering (WWV) is to make it easier for people to volunteer by providing access to information about a wide range of volunteering opportunities throughout the UK and worldwide.

The WWV database enables volunteers to build an on-screen profile of their ideal volunteer placement which is then matched against the requirements of over 1,400 organisations with more than 1,000,000 placements each year throughout the world.

Schools, colleges, universities, careers and connections services, libraries and volunteer bureaux subscribe to the database.

New titles from Guardian Books

The Guardian Media Directory 2007

Now in its seventeenth year, the essential handbook for media professionals, journalists and students features MediaGuardian's unrivalled industry analysis - plus more than 13,000 up-to-date key contacts including email addresses.

MediaGuardian writers and industry experts analyse the state of the media for 2007 - in press, TV, radio, new media, global media, advertising, PR, media law, film, music and more.

Includes updated media contacts for every sector of the industry - including newspaper editors, TV and film producers, radio stations, publishers, record companies, agents, press agencies, lawyers and more.

PLUS: Listings of media courses and training providers, awards, recruitment agencies and diversity organisations together with the advice you need to launch a successful career.

The Guardian Guide to Careers
New Edition

Extensively revised and updated to include completely new features and sections.

Whether you are a school-leaver or graduate, The Guardian Careers Guide helps you find the perfect job.

As well as a traditional A-Z guide of over 200 careers in 25 different industries, this unique guide will show you what challenges and questions you will face if you decide to follow a particular career. Industry experts advise how their particular career sector is changing, what skills are coming to the fore, and what the big issues are: the challenges, the necessary sacrifices to be made and the possible achievements to be had both now, and in the next five years.

PLUS: invaluable, easy to follow tips on how to secure the job, including writing CVs and covering letters; filling in application forms; using recruitment consultants; online job hunting; and preparing for interviews.

The Guardian University Guide 2008

Thinking of taking a degree but not sure what subject to study or where to study it? Need help making the big decisions about higher education in the UK?

The Guardian University Guide is the most fully comprehensive guide on the market. Packed with no-nonsense advice, it guides students through every process, from applications to interviews, accommodation to finances.

The Guardian subject ratings are the most up-to-date on the market and the only ones to be based on the UCAS entry tariffs so that students can judge for themselves which are the best universities available to them.

University profiles written by students already studying at their chosen university completes the picture on what university life is really like.